Acting Out

Your Personal Coach to a Money-Making Career in Television Commercials

by Stuart Stone, CCDA
and Dennis Bailey

Cricket Feet Publishing
Los Angeles

Acting Out: Your Personal Coach to a Money-Making Career in Television Commercials
© 2003 by Stuart Stone, CCDA and Dennis Bailey
First Edition

Cricket Feet Publishing
P.O. Box 1417
Hollywood, CA 90028
phone/fax: 323.871.1331
http://www.cricketfeet.com
publisher@cricketfeet.com
Distributed by SCB Distributors, Los Angeles

Cover design by Fabiana Cesa
Edited by Bonnie Gillespie
Stuart's headshot by Dorothy Goulah
Dennis' headshot by Mary Ann Halpin
Printed in Canada

LCCN 2003103285
ISBN 0-9723019-5-X

Cricket Feet Publishing titles may be purchased in bulk at special discounts for promotional or educational purposes. Inquiries for sales and distribution, textbook adoption, foreign language translation, editorial, rights and permissions, and future edition inquiries should be addressed as above or to publisher@cricketfeet.com.

Cricket Feet Publishing is a registered trademark.

WHAT OTHERS ARE SAYING ABOUT *ACTING OUT*

"As a casting director, I appreciate Stuart's direct approach to commercial acting as a whole. His book is a roadmap that can lead actors to success."

—Joseph Middleton, CSA

"Much like his teaching, Stuart Stone's book is insightful and realistic: guiding actors step-by-step along the path to success in commercials."

—Marnie Cooper, owner, School of Acting, Inc.

"As a casting director, Stuart reveals tangible and useful information which actors usually do not have access to. As a refresher or intro to what it takes to break through, this book is an invaluable tool which I highly recommend."

—Judy Kerr, actor/author/coach

Dedicated to Skyler Stone
and you, the actor who has chosen to venture down the
path into acting.

—Stuart

and

To my parents: John and Shirley Bailey as well as my
tolerant siblings Patrick, Linda, and Michael,
who have learned not to change the channel
when a commercial comes on.

—Dennis

TABLE OF CONTENTS

ACKNOWLEDGMENTS

First and formost, to my family and friends who have believed in and supported me: Edyce Stone, Scott and Stacy Stone, Jeremy Bernard (you make the best burgers), Kelly Jones (for so many many reasons), Milton Stone, Irving and Pauline Wieder, Yetta and Stanley Stone. My deepest appreciation to Mike Hubert for his continuous kind words and unending support. Thank you to the agents, managers, teachers, and actors who provided me with insights as well as confidence. And thanks to my editors and publishers at Cricket Feet Publishing—Bonnie and Keith—for digging the path.

—*Stuart*

Thank you to my indefatigable commercial agents: Neil, Sheila, and Blair, who, with Margaret and Bill, have been wizards at blazing a satisfying commercial path for me.

—*Dennis*

INTRODUCTION

As the 21st century opens, the avenues of employment for the actor are more varied than at any other time in history. The performer can ply his or her trade in a myriad of venues: Stage—Broadway, regional, and waiver; Film—studio, independent, and computer-generated; Television—episodic, cable, and music videos; the Internet; and commercials. All have their distinctions; all have their various appeals. And all use the same basic acting technique for the final performance, just calibrated a bit to best serve each specific category. This guidebook serves to focus on one particular domain: Commercials.

Long considered the "poor relative" of the acting profession, commercials have emerged to become one of the most inventive, cutting-edge, satisfying, and lucrative divisions of the performing career. Many top directors including Ridley Scott and Michael Bay began in commercials; countless famous actors such as Martin Sheen, Melanie Griffith, Brian Dennehy, Andie MacDowell, Wendie Malick, Gene Hackman, James Garner, James Earl Jones, James Whitmore, and Cybill Shepherd join the not so famous (but no less talented) in lending their faces and/or voices to commercials. Working in commercials can be an end in itself, or an exciting supplement to a successful acting career. Whether onscreen, voiceover, radio, television or print, the in-demand commercial actor today commands respect and—thanks to compounding residuals—an enviable income.

But what is the best way to break into the commercial game? How does one adapt the craft of acting to accommodate the commercial parameters? How do you not only find out what category you fit in, but perfect your approach? Which divisions of commercials are the best for you to concentrate on? Do you need to join the actor's unions? Do you need agents? Managers? Expensive pictures and resumés? This guidebook answers these questions while breaking down the mythology of the industry so that any actor can reap the benefits that commercials have to offer. Not only can you be financially successful at a commercial career, but you can also derive genuine artistic gratification beginning with the initial casting process, through the actual shooting, and on to the final result. All it takes is a little time, a little talent, a little focus, a little preparation...

...and this book.

CHAPTER ONE

Getting Started

So, you're an actor. In spite of what everyone's told you, warned you, and predicted for you, you've decided that performing is what you'd like to do with your life. Perhaps you did theatre in school. Maybe you've trod the boards in summer stock or appeared in a student film or two. And now you've decided to go professional and try making some money at it. And you're thinking: What about commercials? Or maybe you're already an established working actor who's decided that supplementing your income might not be such a bad idea. And you're wondering: What about commercials? Perhaps you've made commercials in the past but now you're stuck and haven't been booking lately. And now you're reevaluating: What about commercials?

Well, what *about* commercials? How do you start? What do you do? How can you make such a career choice a viable reality?

Beginning a successful career in commercials is not unlike any other acting venue. A competitive and challenging endeavor, it demands presence, talent, a distinctive look, confidence, and perseverance. You also have to have the correct type of pictures, accurate and informative resumés, agility at improvisation, classes logged in commercial technique, a reliable agent, a varied wardrobe, and a palpable business sense. But in commercials—beyond performing in a part, or assuming a character—you are also selling a product (as well as yourself). It is a skill that has to be honed; it's a talent that has to be developed; it's a knack that has to be mastered.

If you really want to break into the commercial game, actually sit down in front of the television and watch commercials. When you do, you will probably be amazed by the sheer variety offered. Commercials can be clever, funny, informative, heart-warming, slick, all-dancing, all-singing, dopey, bizarre, simple, or complex. Some have real behavior, some odd, and some mannered. Some have words—or copy; others have only action with music under. Some have actors breaking the fourth wall by speaking directly to the audience; others are totally self-contained. And if you look closely you will see that the variety of the ads is matched by the variety of actors: male, female, old, young, beautiful, goofy-looking performers playing an extensive range of roles: business people, parents, kids, friends, lovers, fast-food gobblers, allergy-sufferers, beer connoisseurs, soda guzzlers, potato chip poppers, cereal munchers, pet lovers, car drivers, litigating lawyers, concerned doctors, and product spokespeople. The array is nearly endless.

See what appeals to you. Note what types are selling. Mark what category or categories you think you might be right for. If you believe that you have what it takes, or even if you just want to find out if you do, then it's time to begin.

This guidebook is designed as a roadmap to direct you through to a successful career as a commercial actor. The trip starts in this first chapter and ends with your arrival at the last. Here are your signposts.

- *Getting Started*
- *Commercial Classes*
- *Style, Image, and Wardrobe*
- *Photographs, Retouching, Reproduction, Resumés, and Listings*
- *Home Business Office*
- *Unions*
- *Agents*
- *Acting Techniques Adapted for Commercials*
- *The Audition*
- *The Personal Pep Talk*
- *Booking the Job, Contract Issues, On-Set Etiquette*
- *Making It Happen*

These chapters are designed in such a way that the information in one leads methodically to the other; it is not advised to skip around, jump ahead, or attempt a shortcut. This will only result in lost time and lost money. If, for instance, you should choose to get pictures and resumés before you enroll in a commercial workshop, you may discover that your choices are totally wrong and unusable for your type. Or, should you decide to interview with agents before perfecting what your own personal style and persona are, the prospective agent may be less adept at successfully marketing you. Wasted hours. Wasted dollars.

16—Acting Out

This is a guidebook. You shelled out some bucks for it. Let it do its job so you can do yours.

CHAPTER TWO

Commercial Classes

You don't begin a career as a stockbroker by just showing up on Wall Street and buying and selling shares of IBM; you don't become a painter by picking up a brush and throwing some paint at a canvas; you don't start a law practice by watching reruns of *Perry Mason.* So why do some people believe you can just put your face in front of a camera and—bang—instantly become a successful commercial actor? Yes, every once in a while a commercial will feature a non-professional, man-on-the-street type or a model with no acting experience. However, more often than not, these appearances are strictly one-shot deals. A type, a reaction, or even chiseled good looks only go so far. If you want to achieve longevity in commercials, you'd better know what you are doing.

Acting is a craft requiring skill, technique, and knowledge. It takes practice and diligence to hone it into a successful career. And when an actor decides to also concentrate on commercials, a new list of variables arises: camera ease, type, category, product, likeability, and sincerity. Why not find some professional direction and focus to optimize your chances of booking that job? Why not be confident that you are more masterful than 90% of the actors that have walked into that audition room before you? Instead of relying on hope, rely on craft. The quickest and best way to thoroughly learn the ins and outs of the commercial game is to enroll in a commercial workshop.

For a nominal fee and a few hours, a professional casting director or seasoned commercial actor will take you through the paces of the rigors of auditioning for television commercials. You will learn how to define your type and how to optimize your appeal. You will see what sort of headshots and resumés will show you off to the greatest advantage. You will go through the different types of commercials and learn how to master copy and improvisation techniques. You will hone pantomime and visualization methods. You will find out the differences between stage and camera direction. You will discover secrets about what the client really looks for in an actor. Most importantly, you will get valuable practice time in front of the camera. This facet alone is worth the price of admission to a workshop. Nothing instructs commercial actors more potently or succinctly than showing them actual videotape of themselves auditioning.

The choice you have to make is which type of teacher you feel more comfortable studying with: a casting director or a professional actor. Studying with each has its advantages. Casting directors have insights as to what is required in auditions. They are in the audition room throughout the process and are working from the director's and advertising agency's instructions. They direct the session and understand fully what it takes to book that particular job. A successful actor, on the other hand, may relate in language more familiar to you and instruct from the guidelines of how an actor approaches a role. One viewpoint comes from behind the camera, the other from in front of it. Investigate both and see which approach appeals to you more. Ask actor friends for recommendations. Some teachers will even go so far as to let you audit a class for free to decide if their instructional methods are beneficial to you. There is certainly no harm—and probably much benefit—in taking a class from both and combining the lessons of the two.

In workshops, you will network with other actors as well as the teacher in the pursuit of answers to your questions. Through the instruction—from the best places to go for pictures, to recommendations for other helpful classes, to lists of franchised agencies, to websites to get your pictures on—you end up not only a better commercial actor, you also end up saving money by finding out what works and what doesn't.

Used in conjunction with this guidebook, you will emerge from the classes much more skilled, confident and savvy in your career. Both casting directors and prospective agents look favorably on commercial workshops listed on your resumé. It says to the people in charge that you are taking your career seriously and are intent on doing everything you can to be the best you can possibly be at your craft.

It is important that when you look for a workshop that you get references, as well as find out if the teacher is currently working in the industry. When was the last time they worked? Was it in the field they are claiming to have knowledge of? There are teachers that worked as actors or casting directors or casting associates many years ago and are still holding on to that several years later and are out of touch with the changes that have occurred in the industry. Classes with these people often lead actors to be poorly instructed. This may set you back and teach you techniques that worked in the past but will be hard habits to break so that you can work in today's market.

CHAPTER THREE

Style, Image, and Wardrobe

While the craft of an actor on stage, television, and film demands that the performer delve into subtext and ultimately disappear into the character he or she is portraying, acting in commercials offers a process that is slightly different. In commercials, you must, first and foremost, have a definite perception of who you are. What is your style? What does your look entail? It's important that you be as specifically *you* as you are able. Not only is it your strength, but it's also something no one else in the world possesses. This is your look, your persona. Stand in front of a mirror and take a long, hard, objective look at yourself. Commercials are all about type. When you decide what exact type you are, then you must mold that image into something clear, stylish, intriguing, and marketable.

If style is not your particular strong point, then turn to friends whose taste you trust for advice. Or look in trendy magazines and clothing catalogues to see what is hot or current. When you decide what is your unique look, then fashion it into a sellable commercial type.

What follows are some typical commercial types.

Men

Juvenile—student; kid brother; kid next door; punk.
Teen—student; street-wise; son; athlete; nerd; musician.
Young Adult—businessman; clean-cut; preppy; yuppie; newlywed; young father; neighbor; blue-collar worker.
Adult—businessman; spokesman; teacher; father; neighbor; couch potato.
Senior—spokesman; grandparent; retiree.

Women

Juvenile—student; family member.
Ingénue/Teen—student; daughter; cheerleader; sweetheart; mall-shopper.
Young Adult—businesswoman; newlywed; young mother; neighbor; housewife.
Adult—businesswoman; spokeswoman; housewife; neighbor; mom.
Senior—spokeswoman; grandmother.

Because it is a valuable tool in your profession, a certain amount of the actor's wardrobe is legally tax-deductible. So, get out and hit the mall. If you are on a limited budget and can't afford retail, shop around at second-hand stores or factory outlets. If you are truly among the fashion clueless and have the funds, you may want to consult a color consultant expert or stylist to decide what colors, wardrobe, and image are most advisable for you. And because the expert's fee is a one-time expense (and also deductible), in the long run the session can save you money by making you a more specific and disciplined shopper.

General wardrobe specifications for commercial calls are divided into the following categories.

Casual—general hanging out or knocking-about apparel; maybe khakis or Dockers for men; slacks for women; T-shirts or Izods. Stay away from jeans unless requested.

Nice Casual—what you might wear on a date; sometimes called the "P & G Look" (after Procter and Gamble); for men, an Oxford shirt or sweater and slacks; for women, a blouse and skirt (and get out the iron, for God's sake).

Upscale Casual—tweaked a bit toward the classy; nicer fabrics; a tailored cut.

Upscale—dressy; a tie for men; a designer dress for women; apparel you would send to the cleaners when soiled.

Business/Spokesperson—suits for both men and women.

Hip/Trendy—the newest fashion statement; be prepared for anything from punk (low rider jeans, fake tattoos, and piercings) to cutting-edge, designer-driven (Tommy Hilfiger, Hugo Boss, Donna Karan, Ralph Lauren, Perry Ellis) ensembles.

If you are secure with your look and type, you can adapt it to any of the above categories.

When you are called to audition by your agent, it is usually an assistant giving you your appointment time and wardrobe requirements. Make sure you understand the dress required. The casting director told your agent who told an assistant and the degree of separation may let specific information get lost or misinterpreted. Double check. Don't be put in the position of showing up, for instance, in grunge-wear when eveningwear was requested.

This audition wardrobe should always be ready to wear at a moment's notice. Sometimes you will have more than one call a day and not enough time to keep returning home to change for each different look required. Have a backpack or small valise that you can use to transport your apparel. This will keep your clothes clean and wrinkle-free. Or, even better, if you have a car, keep appropriate audition outfits—business, casual, sporty— stored in your trunk. That way, if you receive a last-minute call while on the road, you will be prepared. Most casting studios have spacious, relatively clean restrooms where talent can change into required wardrobe.

CHAPTER FOUR

Photographs, Retouching, Reproduction, Resumés, and Listings

Photographs

Not only is your 8x10 headshot your official business calling card, but it is also the most vital career-marketing tool you possess. It is an unparalleled weapon in your promotional arsenal; it is literally your ticket in the door. More often than not, the photograph is your first introduction to the professionals who will be selecting you for interviews and auditions—and hopefully—ultimately casting you. Your picture will be one of hundreds that passes the desk of a casting director or agent on any given day. Make no mistake; commercial acting is a very competitive game. If you want that agent, casting director, or director to seriously consider you, you must grab their attention in the instant they spend glancing at your picture. If your headshot is not successful in doing that, then your picture is headed for a slam-dunk into the wastebasket.

Consequently, it's imperative to have first-class, professional photographs. Casting directors, agents, producers, and directors will schedule you for a meeting or an interview because of something indefinably intriguing that they see in your expression, attitude, look, or smile. Always bring an 8x10 picture to each interview or audition; it's the only contact source that people you meet will have to recall you. As your photograph portfolio grows, you will be able to show the interviewer a variety of varying, distinctive representations: body and stunt shots, glamour or model poses, shots of you in character from a film or play, with or without facial hair, and boasting varying hairstyles.

When shopping for the right photographer to take your picture, it is sound business practice to interview three or four. This is not the time to be impulsive. Investigate your options. It's a decision that will have a definite and sometimes long-lasting impact on your career. Although you can find photographers in trade publications, it's even better to solicit advice from other actors or teachers and coaches in the acting business. If someone's 8x10 catches your eye, ask who took the picture. A satisfied customer with a memorable picture is a photographer's best advertising.

When you meet with photographers, don't be shy. Carefully peruse their portfolios. Study their proof sheets to discern the ratio of usable versus unusable shots per roll. Search for the technical quality of each photograph. Is there an energy and likeability caught in the facial expression of the subjects? Are the eyes alive? Is skin tone appealing? Concentrate on pictures of people in your age range with similar facial characteristics and coloring so you can gauge how that person was lit. Avoid photographers with a penchant for overly dramatic lighting or angles. For commercials, you need a clear, clean, uncluttered look. The shot is supposed to sell the person in *front* of the camera, not *behind*. Many photographers shoot both in a studio and outside in various locations. Ask if you can see examples of both and decide which appeals to you. Natural light can be an interesting variation from the standard artificial studio lighting. If you wish, inquire if it is possible to split the session between the two locations. Most photographers appreciate clients who have clear ideas of what they want.

The photographer's personality is also very important. Choose someone you can trust and feel comfortable with. You need to be relaxed to have a fruitful, productive session. You may like someone's portfolio, but if you do not connect with him or her personally, move on. Only choose a photographer who will not only make you look good, but will make you feel good, too. If you feel open and secure with the photographer, the ease will show in your pictures.

Generally, a photo shoot can run from $200 to $600 depending on the reputation and status of the photographer. Many less expensive photographers can be as good as or better than the expensive ones, so do not rely on price alone. Check out their work. If the photographer also does make-up (and many do) check to see if it is included in the fee. It is not necessary to go overboard and pay extravagant sums for your photo session. On the other hand, don't rely on a willing pal with a Kodak Instamatic just to save a few bucks, either. Find a photographer who satisfies your wallet *and* your artistic considerations. Simply said, if the picture gets you an appointment, then the picture is doing its job. It is important to also find if the photographer offers a reshoot if you are unhappy with the way the pictures came out and any other stipulations they may not tell you up front.

Prior to the age of thirty, because of your changing look, you may need new pictures every couple of years. After that, every three to five years will suffice. Although photographs may be your biggest expense, they provide your greatest payoff. This is one of the few without a doubt, guaranteed, worthwhile reasons to invest some serious money in your career.

When you finally do decide on a photographer, use the session to your full advantage. Get plenty of sleep the night before so you are rested and looking your best. Clear the day of the shoot so you can fully concentrate on the task at hand. The most important thing to remember is this: You want your picture to look like you do when you walk into any given audition. We can't stress that enough, so we're going to repeat it. **You want your picture to look like you do when you walk into any given audition, at any time.** Not how you'd like to look, not how you imagine you'd look after a visit to the plastic surgeon, not how your mother tells you how you look when she pinches your cheek, but how you *really* look. So wear things that you usually wear; style your hair as you regularly do. If you do your own make-up, ask the photographer on your first meeting if it will look good in their lighting and on their grade of film. If the photographer is doing your make-up, be sure that the final on-camera result looks like you normally do. Some actors, especially women, feel more secure if a professional make-up artist does their make-up for a shoot. If the make-up person is new to you, make sure you check out their work as well, concentrating on their ability to make actors look natural in black and white photographs.

The session is something you don't do every day—so do what you need to to make you feel comfortable. Bring water and food since you may be there longer than you thought and you want to keep your energy up. Also, women, bring your own make-up, hair dryer, and rollers—even if a make-up artist is hired. Many forget things and it can become a frustration to you. If you need hair gel or styling tools, bring your own.

Below is a list of some of the clothes you might want to bring to your session. Discuss your possible wardrobe with the photographer beforehand for suggestions. Together you should be able to come up with what will work best for the commercial look you desire.

Wardrobe List

Men

Sporty—Izod shirts; T-shirts with or without collars; weathered sweatshirts; colorful parkas; Abercrombie & Fitch or J. Crew logo gear; zip-up cotton jackets.

Rugged Outdoor—plaid or woolen shirts; faded denim shirts; jean jackets; sheepskin, leather, or big, bulky jackets. Also, large, textured sweaters such as ski and fisherman knits jump out nicely in photographs.

Street—tight black T-shirts or tank tops; black, navy, or gray sweatshirts; rough-looking jeans and jackets.

Clean-cut—Oxford-type shirts in subtle colors and patterns; V-neck and crewneck sweaters; non-patterned sports or suede jackets; some good-fitting jeans or pants with a stylish belt; maybe some suspenders; stuff you would maybe find at the Gap, Banana Republic, or Ralph Lauren.

Businessman/Executive—three-piece suit; designer shirt; stylish tie; simple and tasteful; Armani. Hugo Boss. Perry Ellis.

Women

Casual—textured men's shirt; subtly patterned blouses; angora; V-neck, crew neck, and turtle neck sweaters. Vintage and second-hand clothing can give character when anchored with jeans or khakis featuring an array of belts.

Business/Spokeswoman—tweed, patterned, or plain; Donna Karan or Liz Claiborne-type suits; unfussy tailored blouses in light colors; tailored pants or skirts; hose and heels.

Upscale—silk or linen blouses; black sweaters and dresses; off the shoulder, collared, or scoop necklines. Stay away from differing colors on the upper and lower halves of your body—they tend to split you in half. Go for an elongated, svelte look.

Romantic/Sexy—low-cut neckline blouse or dress; lacy or sheer camisole and provocative lingerie; a leather mini-skirt with heels. Remember to bring your own accessories.

With make-up applied, hair fixed, and wardrobe set, it's time for the shoot to begin. Maybe do a few relaxation exercises before the shutter clicks. Perhaps ask the photographer if you can put on some of your favorite music to soothe or energize you. Breathe. Look straight into the lens, eyes animated and full of energy. Personalize the camera as someone you are eager to relate to. Let your guard down and abandon your defenses; be at your most vulnerable. The camera is not only recording your face but your personality.

In the past, commercial 8x10 shots were always simply a black and white close-up on the face—literally a *headshot*. Lately, however, that rigidity has softened. Some actors use an occasional color picture; some investigate sepia, believing the shades make their photos stand out from the pack. Shots from the waist up are also becoming more and more popular. Besides displaying what kind of body type you have, they show a little more character and carriage. Always keep in mind that the picture must be representative of how you will look at any given audition, but feel free to be reasonably creative with the photographer during your shoot.

On a technical note, however, stay away from horizontal headshots. It becomes a hassle when casting directors go through the ritual of flipping through stacks of submissions to stop at a horizontal photo. Instead of stopping to turn your picture to view it properly, many will simply skip over you so they do not have to slow down the speed of going through the submissions. In this case, your attempt to stand out from the pack may get you thrown out of the pack. Also, on certain web-based services, horizontal headshots are not adapted, and will appear sideways on the screen.

When in doubt, remember that no one looks like you and all you need in order to be unique is to capture your essence in a clean, uncluttered, striking photograph. A basic headshot is still, at the end of the day, very acceptable and usually the best choice.

After the shoot is accomplished, your photographer should provide you with developed film and printed proof sheets with up to 36 exposures on each. It is possible to have all the shots done in 4x6 proof prints as well as a CD-ROM of your pictures, but this is usually an added expense. The nominal charge for 4x6 proofs is worth it, since the proofs will be easier to decide upon at that size, than from on a proof sheet. The choice is yours. If you go with proof sheets, the only reliable way to properly view them is through a photographer's loupe, which magnifies each small shot. You can and should buy one at your local camera shop for a few dollars. While you are there, also pick up a grease pencil—which wipes away easily with a tissue—to mark possible choices directly on the proof sheet. Armed with your pencil and loupe, examine the proofs for lighting and focus. Cross out all the ones that are fuzzy or framed incorrectly. Then begin the daunting task of choosing your shots.

First, ask your photographer to pick his or her favorite choices. Corral three or four people for their opinions of which pictures look most like you. It's best to ask people in the business: your acting coach, a working actor, an agent, or casting director. Keep track of each person's picks and then make your choices. Because actors are notorious at choosing photographs that don't look like themselves, pick last so you can see how others perceive you. Blow up your selections into 8x10 borderless (four-way bleed) matte finish masters. Or, if you like, try interesting, artistic borders your photographer, agent or photo lab may suggest.

Take the master 8x10s to three or four people and ask their opinions. Some pictures will be eliminated right away because of flaws that were not perceptible when looking at the proof sheet or 4x6s. Be aware, though, that many of these flaws can be corrected by retouching; a good picture is worth the expense. Next, examine the master prints chosen most by your advisors and figure in your particular favorites. Then have them retouched if necessary and reproduced.

Don't despair if it takes more than one photo session to get the 8x10 you desire. Although it can be very discouraging not to have your pictures come out as you hoped they would, it is not all that unusual, especially on a first shoot. Maybe you like them, but your agent doesn't. Maybe you want to take a scissors to them all. While it's hard not to be emotional about all the time and money spent, try to objectively diagnose what did and what didn't work. Was it you? Were you just not comfortable? Is the photographer's work sub-par? Don't get caught up in the blame game, just educate yourself so that the next session will yield the results you want. Save your money, choose another photographer, and jump in again.

Once you have these shots, and your wallet allows, you can add differing, more specific photos to your portfolio. If you have an impressive physique—male or female—and want to display it, you will need a body-shot picture. Wear some body-fitting clothes such as workout gear, Spandex, dancewear or a bathing suit. If you are adept at sports or stunts, you might desire pictures of you doing your specialty. If you are a male and you want to show off all those hours spent at the gym, try a pose in biking shorts or underwear with no shirt. Do not mail these shots, however. Give them out personally when it is appropriate to the role.

For commercial interviews in some parts of the country (usually not Los Angeles), your agent may want a composite card. These can be three or four shots on one side or a commercial headshot on one side and several commercial-type situation shots on the back (such as horseback riding, biking or skateboarding, tennis playing, barbell lifting, runway walking, fast-food munching, cheerleading, baby-tending, and baseball playing). Such shots should concentrate on different facial expressions—background, location, and situation changes are nice, but secondary. The point is to show your range as a commercial actor.

The following pictures are presented here to demonstrate different types of commercial 8x10s.

Here is a black and white shot where the lighting sets the actor apart from the background, presenting a clear, bright, big energy, full-of-life shot of Jake Harris.

When a casting director is going through pictures, he pulls pictures that not only fit the look and type required for the commercial, but also ones that have energy and likeability. This picture of Brian D. Johnson will jump out of any pile, as it is full of energy.

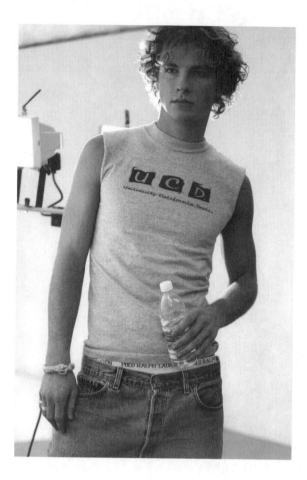

Some commercial actors choose to use a color print modeling shot. This type of picture, favored by models such as Jens Larson, is perfectly acceptable, although some casting directors may pigeonhole an actor who uses this type of picture as someone without a lot of acting experience who depends more on his looks to book commercial work.

Here is an example of a 3/4 type shot. Jake Gates' shot shows a great use of body language, as he leans into the viewer with a great smile and energy.

Christopher Caso's 3/4 shot is on the serious side. This type of picture would more likely be used for theatrical (television and film) submissions, rather than commercial submissions.

This is an example of a horizontal theatrical headshot. Marla Frees uses this shot for theatrical submissions.

Marla's commercial headshot could also be used for theatrical submissions, where appropriate.

Photo Retouching

As stated before, the photos you employ for your headshot should closely represent the real you. Yet, occasionally shadows can appear under the eyes and furrows may pop out on the brow. Annoying zits sometimes dot the skin. Your mouth might be open a little too much or a tooth might look odd catching the light. Maybe your hair looks thin because the light hits it too harshly. Perhaps there's a sweat stain pooling in your armpit or a stray hair that disrupts the look of the photo. So what's to be done? Toss out the pictures you'd like to choose? No. This is a job for a retoucher.

A retoucher is an expert who artistically alters a master print 8x10 to your advantage. And it's cheaper than cosmetic surgery. Your retoucher can advise you according to what your specific needs are; the cost can range from $10 to $50 for an uncomplicated job. As always, get an estimate of the price before proceeding. Work personally with a retoucher. It's valuable for them to meet you and for the two of you to discuss your needs. Many photo labs offer retouching services but usually the clerk marks it and puts it in a stack. When that happens, you aren't a real person to the retoucher. Converse with them personally so they can personally help you be you in your finished photos. Look at some of their work.

Do not take out wrinkles and elements that make you the person you are. You cannot hide them when you go into the audition. You do not want to misrepresent yourself with a picture that, after being touched up, makes you smooth and polished and not like you are on a day-to-day basis—and as you would show up at an audition.

Photo Reproduction

It's important that your original 8x10 master picture be of optimum quality. In the process of mass-production, the picture will lose some facets; it's unavoidable. But you can protect your photo—not to mention the substantial amount of money you've spent thus far—by taking your master, retouched or not, to a duplication lab that specializes in photo reproduction. Just so you are not inadvertently caught short-handed if an interview or audition arises before the lab is finished, it's advisable to Xerox a few copies of your master so you will have something to give an interviewer in a pinch.

Be diligent about protecting your master and negative. If they get damaged you will have to shell out more cash for others. File them carefully away with a sheet of cardboard in a well-labeled 8x10 envelope so they will not only be safe, but readily findable when needed.

A commercial actor goes through large quantities of 8x10s and to save some money, lithographs are an acceptable substitute for the standard, more expensive photographic paper reproductions. It is advisable to shop for a lithographic printing place carefully, as their quality can sometimes be inconsistent. But, because lithographs can fade, wash the master out and weaken your photograph, for theatrical, film, and television submissions it is advisable to have a stack printed on true photographic paper. That way, you can pull a few copies from that pile to be used on special occasions when lithos or 3/4 shots are not the best choice for promoting yourself commercially. Do not make the mistake (outside of a dire circumstance) of Xeroxing your pictures. Although the cost is minimal, the result is tacky. You spent real money on your photographic shoot; don't compromise the effort with a cheesy Xerox copy.

The photographic paper types available at your duplication lab are glossy, matte, or pearl, with or without borders. The cheapest choice is glossy with borders, which is definitely acceptable, although it should be noted that it does not fax well (should such a photo need to be faxed, color-photocopy it before sending). The most expensive photographic paper is pearl and borderless. Sometimes fancy borders cost more, especially the "sloppy" or "full-frame" borders. These borders have the actual sprockets of the film showing and usually must be on your master when you take it to the reproduction house. Again, decide from viewing other people's photos that you like. Or check out the walls of the duplication lab—there are usually hundreds of other clients' 8x10s adorning the walls as advertisements.

Decide how many prints you want run. If you already have agents, they will tell you how many they require to consistently promote you. If you are still looking for an agent, get a short stack of the shot you like. At most reproduction houses, a batch of a hundred is usually the most economical. Don't go wild with spending for multiple shots because a new agent may very well want new pictures taken or new shots mastered from your current proofs and reproduced. Until you do get representation, make certain that you have enough photos to make the rounds. Remember that any picture is better than no picture at all. When you pick up your stack of duplicated photographs, always carefully inspect the negative and prints before accepting them. It's a wise practice to keep the master negatives in your possession. Considering the investment you have made, you will probably take better care of your negatives than anyone else. Of course, if you are lousy at keeping things, then by all means let the lab store the negative for you.

For an added fee, the photo reproduction service can print your name on the front of your pictures. This is an advisable expense because it makes you readily identifiable without turning the photo over to view the resumé and agency information attached to the back. Besides, some submissions are sent without a resumé and a busy agent or assistant can overlook writing your name and the agency on the back of the picture. If that happens, the casting director will have great difficulty identifying you or what agency you are with. If you opt to not have your name printed on the front your picture, make sure you have it on the back in some manner, even if you write it in ball-point pen—and do not leave it up to your agent and their assistants to do it for you! Most agencies have pre-printed stickers with their information on them. If they won't sell them to you from the office, they will tell you where you can purchase them. Get them and slap them on the back of your photo. It is very important to make sure your name and your agency's name is on each and every picture. This is, ultimately, your responsibility. A casting director may not have the time to figure out who you are, and he may never find out who you are. Remember, pictures get put in stacks and shuffled through, perhaps getting separated from their attached resumés. Put contact information on the pictures themselves.

Always keep enough photos and resumés on hand—you never know when your agents are going to run out and call you asking for more. Since it usually takes up to a full workweek to duplicate the photographs, you don't want to ever be caught off-guard. Be forewarned that most duplication places demand at least half payment up-front. Many demand full payment. If at all possible, try to negotiate half up-front in case you are not happy with the work done.

In the printing department, you can have postcards printed with your picture and a space for you to write a message. A postcard is a great tool to send out because the casting director may not open an 8x10 envelope, but with a postcard there is nothing to open—your picture is right in front of them. They also work nicely as note cards to leave with casting directors or any other production people with whom you correspond. Have five hundred or a thousand printed blank and then when you want to print a message, you can just run off whatever you need, or handwrite short "thank you for the interview" notes. Let people on your mailing list know what you are doing with your career or provide any other message in that blank space.

Resumés

Your resumé, like the photo stapled to the other side, is helping sell you. It should represent you in the most professional way possible. The purpose of your resumé is to give the reader a brief description of you and your professional experience, any training and special skills and talents. You must have one to go along with your picture when you are seeking interviews and auditions. In the past, an actor only needed a resumé when pursuing legitimate (or theatrical) acting jobs; now more and more commercial directors demand one as well.

Resumé Format

At the top, centered, put your name in bold letters.

On the left side of center in a column put Weight, Height, Hair (color), Eyes (color).

In the center of the page under your name, include any union affiliations (SAG, AFTRA, AEA).

On the right side, place how to contact you—your agent's name and telephone number. If you don't have an agent yet, put your phone number with an answering machine or message service. Do not put your home address or age range on your resumé.

The bulk of your resumé is comprised of your experience and training. Always list the most recent project first, then the others in chronological order.

Start with the heading: *Films.* Under the heading: left column—film title; center column—billing (starring, supporting or featured); right column—the director (if you list a student film, put the name of the school instead of the director).

Next heading: *Television.* Left column—title of show; center column—billing (star, co-star, guest star, featured); right column—director.

Next heading: *Stage.* Left column—title of play; center column—character name (with billing in parentheses); right column—name of the theatre (unless the director is famous, then list both).

Commercials. Choose between the phrases: *List available upon request* or *Conflicts available upon request.* You don't need to list your commercials. Even if contract periods have expired, a listed product will be suspected of being a conflict by potential employers.

The next heading is where you list your training. Under the heading: *Training,* list the teacher you are studying with currently, then any other acting teachers you have had. You can list any specialty class, such as voice or commercials, and the teacher's name. Last, list your degree and from what college.

Next, you will list your special skills. Under the heading: *Special Skills*, list anything that might make you special: foreign languages, accents, dialects, sports, tap dancing, blading, skate-boarding, computers, stunt work, stunt driving, sharp shooting, pilot's license, CPR, etc.

If you have not yet acted professionally, in lieu of *Film/Television/Stage*, put *Acting Workshop Scenes* and list scenes and characters you have performed in acting class. Then look for ways to earn credits to put on your resumé. Student films and plays are ways for your resumé to grow rapidly. It can take perhaps two years (after obtaining your union cards and agent) for your resumé to reach a fairly comfortable professional place. It does grow! Not only is the process is fun, but you will be gaining invaluable experience while perfecting your craft.

Some copy services will typeset and laser-print your resumé. There are many services that advertise in actor-focused periodicals. If you are computer savvy, save some money by typesetting and laser or bubble-jet printing your own resumé. For a clean look, your resumé should be trimmed to 8x10 to fit on the back of your 8x10 picture. Have just a few resumés photocopied each time (you'll be adding credits often) unless you're sending out a large mailing.

Attach the resumé back-to-back to your picture, facing out. Use double-stick tape, spray glue, or staples. When you staple, do it from the picture side and hide the staples in the borders so they won't draw the viewer's eye away from your face. Place two on top and two on the bottom about two inches from the left side so when a three-hole punch is used, the picture and resumé will go into the punch easily.

It's not a bad idea to keep pictures, resumés, and a roll of double-stick tape or stapler in a zippered briefcase in your car. You may get a job because your pictures and resumés are with you.

The following pages contain examples of resumés. The placement of commercial and theatrical agent logos is up to you. You may want to have two separate resumés: one with your theatrical agent's logo, the other with your commercial agent's logo. Some people elect to include a manager's logo as well. The choice is yours!

Name, height, weight, eye color, hair color, etc., can all be laid out in a variety of ways, although the following structure seems to work best and is industry standard.

Jake Harris

Height:	5'9-1/2"	Hair:	Brown
Weight:	160#	Eyes:	Brown

Film

No I'm Free Balling	Principal	Dir. John Boyd

Television

The Howitt Twins (pilot)	Principal	Tom Lynch Prod.
The Andy Dick Show	Featured	Mulligan/MTV
The Tonight Show	Featured	NBC
Jessica Andrews Video	Principal	DreamWorks
MADD PSA	Featured	MADD

Theatre

Fiddler on the Roof	Fyedka	Wilco County Thtr.
The Miser	Anselme	Wilco County Thtr.
The Toys Take Over Christmas	Capt. Toy Soldier	Wilco County Thtr.

Commercials

Conflicts available upon request.

Training

Marnie Cooper School of Acting	Los Angeles
Stuart Stone Commercial Workshop	Los Angeles
N. K. Axelrod, Rocky Mtn. Talent Pool	Los Angeles
Pato Hoffman Film Workshop	Austin, TX
JoEdna Boldin Audition Technique	Austin, TX
Donise Hardy Casting Workshop	Austin, TX
Linda Major, Acting for Stage	Austin, TX

Special Skills

Baseball; Football; Horseback Riding (Western); Volleyball; Roller Blading; Ice Skating; Snow Skiing; Snorkeling; Bowling

Agent Logo   Manager Logo

Your Name
Union Affiliation

Height:	in ft., in.	Hair:	color
Weight:	in lbs.	Eyes:	color

Film

Title	Billing	Director/Prod. Co.
Title	Billing	Director/Prod. Co.
Title	Billing	Director/Prod. Co.

Television

Show Title	Billing	Prod. Co./ Network
Show Title	Billing	Prod. Co./ Network
Show Title	Billing	Prod. Co./ Network

Theatre

Play Title	Role Played	Theatre Name
Play Title	Role Played	Theatre Name
Play Title	Role Played	Theatre Name

Commercials
Conflicts available upon request.

Training

Instructor, School (Technique Studied)	Location
Instructor, School (Technique Studied)	Location
Instructor, School (Technique Studied)	Location

Special Skills
Skill list (including sports, languages, dialects, accents, dance styles, vocal ability and range, odd abilities)

Listings

Academy Players Directory

The *Academy Players Directory* is a series of books containing actors' photographs, their resumés, their representation, and the avenues available to reach them. Nearly every agent, producer, director, and casting director has the *Directory* on a shelf in their offices. It is an invaluable tool in tracking down a certain actor, or viewing an entire category of actors for a certain project. By thumbing through the book, or logging in online, a director or producer can point to an actor that they believe the casting director should call in for a session. Or the casting director can view the directory looking for a face or a type that wasn't included in the agent's submissions. It is very important for your picture to be in the *Academy Players Directory*. And at a reasonable fee of about $75 a year, there is no reason for you not to be included in the ranks.

The directory is sectioned into eight easily-perused categories:

- *Leading woman*
- *Ingénue*
- *Character & Comedienne Female*
- *Leading Man*
- *Younger Leading Man*
- *Character & Comedian Male*
- *Child Female*
- *Child Male*

For inclusion in the *Academy Players Directory*, you must have a union-franchised agent, a personal manager, or belong to one of the three actor's unions (SAG, AFTRA, AEA). There are specific registration periods. The base fee is $75 a year for one picture in one category. Should you want two photos, the price climbs to $85, three photos will run you $95. In the past you could renew per every four months. Now you can only renew yearly. If you feel as an actor that your type spans two categories—that, for instance, you do leading man and character roles—it might be advantageous to shell out a little extra money to include yourself in both slots. You are able to log-on to the website at any time, free of charge, to update your resumé.

Online and CD-ROM Casting

Although, for the most part, casting is still done by 8x10 hard copy photo submissions to casting directors, the computer is affording some high-tech venues for the actor. For a fee, a picture, resumé, representation, and even a short video can be burned onto a compact disk and integrated into a non-public CD-ROM system that is distributed to casting directors. The Internet also offers opportunity for displaying your own website, available to the public. These venues are constantly evolving, much like the high-tech world of computers itself. Check to see what is currently the most up-to-date method of gaining online exposure. Ask other actors, not online sales reps.

As these systems become more and more user-friendly, casting directors are beginning to use online casting services. Confer with your agent to decide if you should join the cyber revolution and computerize your picture and resumé. Do your homework as to not spend money needlessly on sites not used frequently enough to justify the cost to join.

Personally designing your own website or CD-ROM could very well be, in itself, another artistic outlet for your talents. Be reminded though, that if you do elect to use this service, for safety reasons, never list your home phone or address.

Clearly, casting directors do not have the time to click on every actor's personal website. Still, the venue can be very helpful in a situation where an agent or manager is recommending talent in a pitch and mailing or messengering the actor's headshot and resumé is an unsatisfactory option. The casting director—usually in the middle of a session in which casting of a particular role is proving to be a challenge—can immediately surf to the proposed actor's website and view a picture, resumé, and maybe even a short voice recording or demo reel.

Photos, resumés, listings—it's all about getting your face out there. And making sure that it's a face that people want to see.

CHAPTER FIVE

Home Business Office

Most performers like to think of themselves as artists, and indeed, they are. But, unfortunately, that label sometimes allows the actor to be lackadaisical about the business side of his or her career: the nuts and bolts, the structure, the groundwork, and the footwork. As an actor you are, to a certain extent, self-employed. This is your business. As an old pro once memorably quipped, "It's not called show *art*, it's called show *business*." This is especially true of the commercial actor.

In order for your artistic side to excel, you have to hone your practical and organizational side as well as study your craft. That means setting up an office of sorts. Some are lucky enough to have a separate space they can fashion into a workplace; others have to make do with an alcove or corner in the kitchen or bedroom. Wherever your office is situated, you'll need a desk for either file folders or filing drawers, a private phone line and answering system—machine, voicemail, or service—a fax machine, and a computer. Throw a picture or two up on the wall; maybe an inspirational adage on a plaque. Get a comfortable chair. Make your office a place you like spending time. Even if the rest of your life is an unstructured, unholy mess, keep your business office uncluttered and operational. It will pay off.

The Desk

It doesn't matter if it's a real desk or makeshift. An old kitchen table, or some planks resting on short filing cabinets will do. On top should be space for your phone, answering machine, computer, and fax machine with enough elbowroom leftover to write. Drawers would be nice as you'll need storage for stationery, appointment and audition log book (which you should carry with you whenever you are out on a call), business envelopes, 9x12 manila envelopes, postage stamps, networking card file, an in/out call log (a great reference tool if you lose a number), and pens and pencils. Keep the desk clean so you know where everything is when you need it.

The Filing System

Devise a filing system that makes sense to you. If you don't have a filing cabinet, use an accordion file divided into appropriate subtitles. If you are not skilled at organization, follow the headings listed below.

Advertising/Promotion—Publicity on yourself
Bank Statements
Correspondence
Income Statements
Master Headshots and Negatives
Personal—Passport, Social Security Card, Birth Certificate

Photographs

Receipts—An actor can legally deduct anything that pertains to the career—movie and play tickets, videos, business dinners, clothing used for auditions, stationery, printing, postage, make-up, haircuts, coaching sessions, VCR, photographs, copying, etc. Keep them all in order for tax time.

Resumés

Reviews

Phones

It cannot be emphasized enough that you must have your own personal phone line. Do *not* share it with a roommate, your loved one, or even your spouse, no matter how frugal you are. It will not only put a strain on your living arrangement, friendship, or marriage, but it might also compromise your career. The only thing responsible for taking a phone message for you should be your machine, service, or voicemail. A single appointment can mean a change in your career and thousands of dollars. Don't put someone else in the position of seriously screwing that up.

Most phone companies have voicemail, which automatically takes a message if your phone is not answered. The additional charge is added to your monthly phone bill. The only drawback to voicemail is that unlike an answering machine, you cannot monitor incoming calls. Call waiting—a beeping that signals that another call is coming in when you are on the phone—is also available. If you are on the phone—or the Internet—a great deal, call waiting is essential. You don't want to frustrate an agent with an appointment (or any business caller) with a busy signal.

Answering Machines

If you decide on an answering machine instead of voicemail, be certain that it is activated by all push button tones so you can retrieve your messages. Buy a machine that has unlimited length on the incoming message, or that is voice-activated. You don't want your machine inadvertently cutting off someone in the middle of an important message. The outgoing message, on the other hand, should be short, concise, and free of annoying cuteness. Save your creativity for the camera—don't do your funny routines on your answering machine. It will make callers want to throttle you. When agents, for instance, call with an appointment, yours is only one of the many calls they have to make at the end of the day. If they have to listen to all their clients do endless comical riffs on their machines, their heads will explode. Just say your name and number so the callers know they got the right person, and tell them to leave a message at the tone. Answering machines are everywhere these days. You don't have to leave endless instructions for the caller.

And when you're on the other end of the equation—phoning and getting someone's answering machine—say your name and phone number at the very beginning, and then your short and succinct message. That way, if their machine cuts you off, they have your name and number from the top. If you want, leave your number also at the end as another precautionary measure. And it's an important practice to leave your telephone number with every message, even if you believe they already know it. Many times people will be away from their phonebooks when they retrieve their messages. If you want a quick return on your call, make it easy for the other person to do so. Never leave a beeper number for someone to return your call. It just makes more work for the person you are calling. They have to beep you and then they have to wait for you to call them back. Wasted time. Business people get cranky about their time being wasted—and rightfully so.

During business hours, check your machine at least every two hours. Make sure that your machine has the feature where you can set the machine to answer all calls on the second ring when you have messages and on the fourth ring when you do not. That way, you can save yourself money from pay phones or cell phones when calling in for your messages. If your phone rings a full four times, hang up—it means that you have no messages.

Beepers

Because a commercial actor is sometimes on the road all day long running from one commercial audition to another, a beeper is one way to keep in touch when you can't call in as regularly as you should. The beeper number should only be used for business purposes. Buy one with a light or vibration signal so that it will not disturb others around you in a casting call or on the set.

Some beepers come with a voicemail option. Although a bit more expensive per month, many find the added convenience for the caller is worth it. Besides entering their number, the callers can leave messages. You, in turn, are paged with your own beeper number and can answer the messages when you are free to do so.

You may find that your voicemail system offers a beeper option as well. If you elect to have both, link them to the same number.

Cell Phones

Until only recently, cell phones were reserved for emergencies—traffic jams or automobile mishaps. Now, everyone and his dog has a cell. They are, to be sure, the most convenient of the out-of-office communication devices. No more looking for a pay phone in vain; no more waiting until you get home to retrieve your messages. As their popularity has blossomed, so have the options. Some have built-in mini-computers and even link to the Internet. No longer just the playthings of the rich, these mobile phones have lowered enough in cost to make them affordable to almost everyone who desires them. A cell phone can be the actor's best friend. They seriously reduce the risk of your missing notification of a last minute audition or callback. They are also invaluable should you be running late for an audition, or if you find yourself hopelessly lost. When you are on the set, they can be your only link to the outside world.

Unfortunately, while cell phones have proliferated quickly in the past few years, appropriate phone etiquette has not kept pace. We have all been behind the oblivious bonehead dialing in busy traffic, weaving dangerously from lane to lane. Or sat next to the moron talking into a cell phone at the top of his lungs in a restaurant or movie theatre. If you have a cell phone, use a little common-sense courtesy when using it. Don't sit in the waiting room of a commercial audition with your cell shoved in your ear chatting to a friend because you are bored. It is beyond rude; it is downright disrespectful. Other actors are trying to do their job filling out forms or concentrating on copy. If you've got verbal diarrhea, go into the bathroom. Or the hallway. Or the street. If you are at a job—or attending a play or a film—where a personal ringing cell phone is not allowed, make sure you adjust your phone to vibrate mode. If you are in an area with poor reception, it might be best to invest in a beeper. Actors have lost jobs because they were unreachable when called to return to a last-minute third or fourth callback. Don't lose a booking to another actor just because they had a more-effective way of being reached. If you decide that a cell phone will be your primary connection while on the road, it's not a bad idea to also retain a beeper as a backup. Actors turn off their phones during auditions and forget to turn them back on. A beeper on silent vibrator mode willalways alert you that you have a call to return.

Fax Machines

Like the cell phone, the fax machine has become an invaluable tool for the working actor. For television and film roles, sides to study before the audition—once available from one's agent—are now only obtainable from services such as ShowFax, SidesExpress, or other such companies. When a commercial is especially copy-heavy, those sides are also available on those sites the day before sessions. A yearly fee is charged to get these appropriate sides faxed to you. Some grumble that it is yet another way to financially gouge the actor, but at this point there is, unfortunately, no other avenue to receive the material. Production companies also like to fax information about a job booked—location, time, work detail, etc. That way they can trust that you got the right information.

If you don't have a fax machine, your local office supply, copy service, or stationery store will usually have a 24-hour sending and receiving service for a nominal fee. Also, many computers have built-in modems that enable faxes being sent. The computer has to be continually on and connected to a phone line in order to receive faxes.

Computers

Like it or not, we are living in the age of the Internet. You can network and surf through more websites applicable to the actor than can possibly be mentioned in this book. There are support systems, online casting services, information services, map services, and even movie time guides. You can compose your own resumé on your computer, updating it as it changes. And although the quality isn't nearly as good as professional reproduction houses, you can also print out your headshot in a pinch. You can even design your own acting website, complete with 8x10 and list of credits. As mentioned above, your computer can be programmed to receive faxes.

If you are unable to afford your own personal computer, some are available at your local library. In major cities, coffee houses also provide computers with Internet service along with your cappuccino. Maybe you have a friend or acquaintance who is upgrading their system and wants to get rid of their old computer. Check the classifieds for previously owned PCs. An old computer is better than no computer.

Business and Promotional Picture Cards

Although you can store you business cards in your desk drawer, make sure that they are also where they will do the most good—on your person: your wallet, your pocket, your purse, your backpack, your car. Pass them out liberally. You never know when one might pay off. When you hand yours to a business contact, ask them theirs. It eliminates the need for pens and scrap paper and the awkward scribbling down of numbers. It is a professional touch that goes a long way toward exemplifying that you serious about your career. You can have 500 rudimentary but attractive cards with your name and number produced for as little as $20. If you want to be creative, add a splash of color and your miniaturized headshot.

Collate collected business cards in a simple filing system in your business office. Notate the nature of your meeting, the details, the outcome, and the possible future. Your being familiar with people you've met will impress them upon a second encounter, and may result in an employment opportunity for you in the future.

Mailing List and Card File

Your collection of business cards will be the foundation of a contact program and mailing list that can be put on either 3x5 cards or your computer. List all the people you have come into contact with, and attach their cards, with a specific annotation about the encounter. Should you run into them again, or learn something about them, add it to the data.

Combine these names into a potent mailing list. When you book a commercial or get cast in a production, let these influential people know what you are doing by sending a postcard. Work begets work.

Appointment Book

This is the bible for the working actor. Keep it with you always. It is the outline for your working life: your appointments, your classes, your rehearsals, your workouts, your lunches, your business dinners, the movies and plays you've attended. Make sure it has a pen or pencil inside so that you can jot down names and numbers of those who have no business cards.

There are many types of personal appointment books out there such as Filofax, Daily Runner, Day Planner, and Franklin Covey Planners. For clarity, choose one that has a full page for each day. Write down everything the day holds—and your reaction to the events. List purchases for tax purposes. If you are working out of town, chart all your meals and expenses and travel for end-of-the-year deductions.

When you have a clear, concise appointment book, you will find that your schedule runs smoother—any conflicts appear there in black and white. You can see if appointments are too close together to successfully manage. If you are more gadget-inclined, the new electronic Palm Pilot Systems might be beneficial to you. It is essentially a computer-chipped appointment book.

Passport

It is imperative—especially for the commercial actor—to have a current passport. Many commercials are shot in foreign lands and travel regulations demand that the actor have a valid passport. Overseas commercials are notorious for being cast quickly. Since it can take a few weeks to process a passport, should you have one when another actor under consideration does not, you will get the booking. New passports run about $60, with renewals at $40. If you need a passport quickly, for an extra $35, one will be sent to you in three working days.

Passports can be obtained at the Passport Agency at your local federal courthouse, or any United States

Post Office, but you have to have two 2x2 inch photos of your face, proper official identification, and USA citizenship verification. The Department of State's Internet site is www.travel.state.gov. It lists passport forms and post office acceptance facilities. Or you can dial 900-225-5674 24 hours a day for passport information.

Maps

The Internet has many sites such as Mapquest.com or Yahoo.com, which can help you preplan your travel to any audition. If you live in Los Angeles, the *Thomas Guide* is an invaluable source for correct travel. Don't rely on your agents to give you correct directions to any audition— their job is to get you the audition, not get you to it. You should not call a casting director's office for directions.

Hidden Key

We don't mean to sound like your mother here, but keep a magnetic box hidden under the chassis of your automobile containing your house and car key. You don't want to be locked out of your house or your car when you desperately need to get to an audition. It's not a bad idea to keep another one in your wallet or purse.

Post Office Box

If you are concerned about privacy or security matters, you might want to look into procuring a P.O. Box. That way, all your business mail goes to somewhere other than your home. And every time you list your P.O.

Box as your address on a form at an audition, it doesn't matter who sees it.

Although all this business compartmentalization may sound a little overly anal or nitpicky at first, the organizational elements will make your auditioning life so much easier. Actors don't have the usual 9-5 structure to their lives; it's important to find order and clarity where you can.

CHAPTER SIX

Unions

Many actors just starting out rush to find a way to get into the actor's unions. Membership in the unions signifies a coming of age, clout, and legitimization for most performers. The three major organizations are Actor's Equity Association (AEA) for the stage; the Screen Actor's Guild (SAG) for film; and American Federation of Television and Radio Artists (AFTRA) for video tape and radio. The commercial actor relies on SAG and, to a lesser extent, AFTRA. Since AFTRA's jurisdiction is of concern mostly for voiceovers or radio spots, we will concentrate here on the Screen Actor's Guild.

There are two ways to join SAG as a commercial actor. You can attempt to enter by getting vouchers from doing extra work. Vouchers are what you are given if you are a non-union actor and you work as a union extra on a union job. A production company has to hire a particular number of union extras before they can hire non-union actors (who get paid less than the union extras). If a union member does not show up, a non-union extra may be upgraded and get a voucher. Once you have acquired three vouchers you are allowed to join the union. Initiation fee is around $1300.

The second way into SAG is by booking a principal role in a commercial. Once you have your first union commercial, you are eligible to join SAG. Initiation fee is still around $1300.

Our advice is this: chill. It's not imperative for beginners to become union members. Many people think that an agency won't represent them if they are non-union. *Not true.* You may interview with an agency that feels your look is needed in that office and they may get you work, regardless of your union status. An agent may tell you they won't rep you until you are union, but more often than not, that is merely an easy excuse not to take on new, untried talent. Many top agents have non-union actors and are aware that if a non-union actor is sent on an audition and hired for a job, the casting director or advertising agency will write what's called a Taft-Hartley letter to the Screen Actor's Guild. When that occurs, you have thirty days to work as many jobs as you want; after that time period you are considered a "must-join" and will have to pay the initiation fee on your next SAG job. You can, however, do non-union jobs until you join the union.

If this is the position in which you find yourself, you would be advised to gather $1300 and deposit it away in a savings account to accumulate interest until you shoot your second SAG job. Then, when the time comes, you will have the money to formally join—not to mention an added bit of interest to buy yourself a celebration dinner or nice gift. But until that happens, it is best to bide your time. So many actors think that being a member of the union will open agency doors and get them to procure work for you. It is not true. Although the unions are great protection for working actors everywhere, and their benefits cannot be underestimated, union membership in and of itself does not guarantee employment. Statistics show that thousands of union actors do not work—so why dig into your pockets to shell out initiation fees and bi-yearly dues until you absolutely have to?

When you do join, it is important that you carefully read the rules in the contract book and understand how you get paid and for what you get paid. There is a flat rate for an eight-hour shoot day; there is a payment schedule for overtime as well. Compensation for working in hazardous conditions, meal penalties, travel, *per diem* (money for meals when you are out of town), and various other bumps in pay are also chronicled. Circumstances vary with each new contract negotiation, so be responsible and know the parameters of your employment. Even if you have high-powered representation, and are under the protective umbrella of a union, look out for yourself. Do not leave your livelihood to chance no matter what you get paid. Always remember that you are, essentially, a business. You get paid for how you are used. Educate yourself and be responsible in your career. Your agent is not on the set with you. Should you be unaware of something you could be getting paid for—something clearly delineated in the SAG guidelines or in your production contract—then, sadly, it is you who loses out.

CHAPTER SEVEN

Agents

Once you obtain an outstanding headshot and construct a potent resumé, you are ready to begin the important process of searching for an agent. Agents are your official representatives in the commercial business. They get breakdowns from casting directors specifying characters needed for a commercial and then, in turn, submit appropriate actors from their talent pool to the casting director. Because actors do not have access to Breakdown Services, you cannot submit yourself to casting directors for an audition. That's why you need an agent as your professional go-between. Agencies make a 10% commission on whatever you make—and if you make nothing, they make nothing. Consequently, until you book a job, they are covering and paying for all their expenses to submit you. It's a classic leap of faith situation; and one of the reasons they carefully scrutinize potential actors for their agency. Should they choose to represent you, take it as a compliment—they are banking that you will make money.

The following are a few ways to get an appointment with an agent.

A General Submission—this is where the actor mails packets of pictures and resumés with a concise cover letter to a variety of commercial agents. If this is the route you choose, it is highly recommended that you seriously investigate which agencies are right for you. Some may handle mostly character-types; others might have many beginners who do not book a lot. One could have a reputation for strong actors, while another boasts a roster of varied talent that works all the time. Some are large firms with enormous clout; some are small—or boutique—offices that pride themselves on individual care. Some specialize in voiceovers; others focus on print work; most concentrate on television spots. Ask around. Find out the viable differences (and how they apply to you) from actor friends or people in your commercial workshop class. Cross-reference this information with lists of union-franchised agencies available at your local theatrical bookstore. This initial groundwork will save valuable time by narrowing your list of appropriate agencies.

Be advised, though, that agencies receive hundreds of submissions per month through the mail alone. Your envelope will get opened, but it may take a week or two because mailed submissions are not an agent's priority. Their priority is getting their current clients work. When your submission is reviewed, however, the agent will look for what he or she deems as the "commercial appeal" of the particular actor seeking representation. If you have done a commercial, mention it in your cover letter. It will maximize your chances of being called in for an interview. If time goes by without you hearing anything back, do not be presumptuous and phone the agency to see if they have received your envelope. Assume that the Post Office did its job and that if the agency wants to meet you, you will get a call.

Recommendation of a Friend—agents respect and value referrals that come from existing clients within their agency. Make sure, though, that when you ask another actor friend to recommend you to his or her agency, that the actor has a strong, fruitful relationship with that agency. You don't want to be put in the awkward position of being referred by an actor that an agency is unhappy with or even perhaps is about to release.

Recommendation of a Casting Director—many agents will confess that they pay special interest to referrals from working casting directors. They are the people that hire the talent and their knowledge and perception is highly regarded. This is yet another reason to take a commercial workshop and meet the casting directors that teach them. If a casting director knows and likes your work, he or she may recommend you to an agency.

Recommendation of an Acting Teacher—like a casting director, an esteemed acting teacher has a sense of which students might make good commercial types. Their opinions often carry weight with many commercial agents.

Through Work—an agent may have seen you in a waiver play, showcase, film, episodic guest shot, or a commercial and wish to meet with you to discuss representation. Make sure you are easily found through your credits or through SAG.

As in any business, there are some organizations that are better than others and so it is with talent agents. And, unfortunately, some of the larger, more prestigious and influential agencies may get a little more initial attention. If a casting director has the time and is willing to open the picture packages from all agencies, then you have a chance of being seen if your representation is one of the smaller agencies. However, pictures are usually received near the end of the day and have to be opened and gone through and appointment times given out before 6:30pm when the agencies close and the next day is casting. In the midst of this crunch time, some casting directors will often opt to give the top agents the session times for their clients first, believing that it's a safer bet that these actors might be better than those from a lesser agency. Yet, what may be a weak agency to one may be perfectly fine to another. Do your homework and check things out. Ask other actors, casting directors, and people in the business.

What makes some agents stand out above others is their ability to have an eye for talent and see the commercial in their head as it might be on TV. With that vision crystallized, they can provide the appropriate talent from within their office. For instance, let's say the part calls for a 35 year-old athletic dad type. If an agent sends a portly bearded man just because he is 35, the submission makes a casting director wonder about the agent and/or his talent pool. A top agent will send in the men who fit the breakdown and who would typically appear on such a commercial. The one agent only had a partial connection to the talent asked for, and that was age; the look was way off.

Competitive agencies usually handle a more varied stable of talent with not only a marketable look but also training and experience on acting jobs. But, that being said, if you are just starting out, there is no sense in digging in your heels and refusing to meet with anyone but the top commercial agencies in town. Take as many meetings as you can with whomever you can. And the bottom line for the beginner is this: any agent is better than no agent. Your contract with them is only for a year, not a lifetime.

When you get an appointment with an agent you should call and confirm the night before, for a morning appointment, and the morning of, for an afternoon appointment. This effort will show them you are responsible. Many actors forget the business part of the equation; your professionalism will set you apart from the actor wannabes. Dress like you would on a general commercial call—with a leaning towards upscale casual. Avoid perfumes or colognes. Bring an up-to-date picture and resumé with you. If you have a demo reel of your commercials, bring that as well. Arrive twenty minutes early to secure a parking space and find the office. Do *not* be late. And call if you have any problem keeping your appointment. The agent is taking time from his or her busy schedule to meet with you. Do not keep them waiting. A pissed-off agent makes for a piss-poor meeting.

Once you arrive at the office, make a concerted effort to be genuinely friendly to everyone. The receptionist is the first contact and will often comment on the actor to the agents. If you rub them the wrong way it can have a detrimental affect on you. You never know who the person is in the reception chair—the agency owner's niece, or perhaps a junior agent filling in for a sick receptionist. So be polite, smile, sit patiently, and wait. Do not use the opportunity to pull out your cell phone and chat away until you are called into the inner offices.

When you go into the agent's office you sometimes will meet with all the agents in the department that you will deal with on a daily basis. Some agents divide the talent and so you might meet only one agent (or point agent) and once you are signed by the agency you will be introduced to everyone. Meetings are usually laidback and stress-free, as the agent wants the actor to be comfortable. Remember this: most agents reveal that an actor will make an impression—good or bad—within the first minute of the meeting. So be relaxed and articulate and charming from the minute you walk through the door.

You have been brought in for a few reasons. First, the agent wants to assess your likeability. There is nothing worse than an actor with an attitude or one who is introverted or painfully shy. Second, they will want to know if you are a good commercial type. You will be asked what commercials you have done and who cast the spots. Never downplay spots you may have done—"It was just a regional" or "I didn't have any lines" or "I was just an extra." Be proud of your work. You might also be quizzed about what existing relationships you have with casting directors and if you have taken any commercial workshop classes. You will probably be asked to do a cold reading of some commercial copy as well. Many actors with little commercial experience will sometimes unconsciously steer the conversation to their theatrical experience—which the commercial agent is, unfortunately, not particularly interested in. Remember that you are in the meeting to sell yourself as a *commercial* actor. If you have no commercial experience of which to boast, then simply say that you've decided to try commercials because you're a good actor and want to branch out—and that you are convinced you would be good at it. While your work background is important, if you are just beginning, being compelling, marketable, and exciting goes a long way as well. Following the interview, in a decidedly non-pushy way, make sure you know what the agent wants you to do next—should you wait for a call or should you call them? They will let you know their office's particular protocol.

There is only one real reason an actor gets accepted into an agency and that is because the actor is marketable. Agents are like salespeople who sell their products (actors) to buyers (casting directors). If they like you and think you are sellable, then they will represent you. You will not be extended representation, however, if the agent feels that it will negatively impact other clients in your particular category. Their allegiance is to their current roster (as it should be) and, if bringing you into the office means that one of their actors may lose an audition opportunity, then you will be turned down, even if you are likeable and marketable. Sometimes, if they believe that you are lacking in certain areas (poor cold reading techniques, little training) they might suggest that you get into a class, get a little experience and then perhaps come back to re-interview.

Once you are invited to join an agency, you will sign union contracts (SAG and AFTRA) that will last for one year. In return, the agent will support your commercial acting pursuits and work hard for you because, again, the office only makes money when you work. Signed actors should show initiative, establish a friendly relationship with the office, be personable, pleasant and responsible as well as professional.

Just because you've been signed by an agency does not mean you can become complacent. If an actor is lazy and non-committal about his or her career, or goes for extended periods without providing headshots, or doesn't check phone messages or confirm appointments, then that actor's days are definitely numbered at the agency. Agents have no interest in working hard for actors who have no interest in working hard for themselves.

On the other hand, if you are dissatisfied with your agent's work, you should call them on the phone to set up a meeting. Sometimes a simple discussion can smooth out any concerns you might have. If that proves ultimately unsuccessful, you can terminate the contract with written notice within the initial 151 days of the contract if 120 consecutive days have passed without a bona fide offer of employment.

The point is, an invigorating, dedicated, and mutually respectful relationship should exist for both the actor *and* the agent for the partnership to be genuinely fruitful.

CHAPTER EIGHT

Acting Techniques Adapted for Commercials

As varied as acting techniques can be, they all are designed to help the actor create a successful performance. While the process, at the core, is generally the same, the venues in which an actor can be employed are not. Just as performing onstage differs slightly from film, acting in commercials needs a bit of subtle calibrating as well. Technique for a successful commercial audition and performance takes the standard acting percepts and adjusts them specifically to the commercial genre. If you apply what you learned in commercial workshops and combine it with the following techniques, you will finesse the work in the audition room most effectively no matter what the type of commercial.

Types of Commercials

The commercial world is divided into a few categories—print, radio, voiceover, and television.

Print

Modeling photography found in magazines, newspapers, posters, or billboards come under the heading of print work. Many agencies have a print department; others specialize in it. There are no residual payments in print work; you get paid hourly for the photo session. And there is no union for models and actors who work in the print world. Instead of a regular 8x10 photo, an actor specializing in print uses what is called a zed card—a composite shot featuring different guises and poses.

Voiceovers

These spots concern radio commercials, narration over television advertisements, and cartoon characters. If you believe you have an especially distinctive voice, then perhaps you might want to investigate this aspect of the commercial business. Find out if your agency has a voiceover department. Your main tool as voiceover talent is your demo reel. This is a professionally-recorded audiotape or CD featuring your vocal talents. Be mindful, though, that voiceovers are fairly difficult to break into—it is a very select industry in which you can arrive in a bathrobe to do the job. Looks do not matter.

Television

When most people think of commercials, they think of television. It is the branch of commercials on which most agencies and actors concentrate. It is also the primary focus of this guidebook. Pay for commercials is typically a day rate with residuals paid each time the commercial airs.

Television advertising can run the full gamut of forms: one person, no dialogue; two people or more, no dialogue; speaking directly to the camera; and full dialogue between actors. In each case, it's your acting skill that is vital to booking the job.

Should you be required to be just a face for the commercial, you might be asked a specific question during the audition to give the client and director a clear idea of who you really are. They are looking for personality: someone confident and likeable. So relax, have fun and be expressive and creative with your answer. Do not worry about the length of your answer—thirty seconds to one minute is usually a perfect answer time frame. The more creatively and naturally you respond, the better.

If asked, say, what is your favorite sandwich, don't merely reply, "Tuna," and leave it at that. The aware actor will realize that the more he speaks and the more personable he is, the better his chances of being memorable become. Talk about how you would make your favorite tuna sandwich—what kind of bread, what condiments, how much mayo, is there a pickle on the side, what about maybe some potato chips? Keep up with the specifics until the casting director tells you to stop. Remember to be alive facially and vocally as you describe these details. Anybody can ramble on; it's the personality and expression with which you talk that will make the difference.

When the spot has no dialogue, improvisational and pantomime skills can be essential. Let's say, for instance, the audition calls for you to sit at a computer and act as if you are busily working. Most people will come in, sit down and simply mime typing away.

However, a prepared, trained actor will make a lot more out of the situation. Picture a desk familiar to you, the type of computer, the text of what you are typing. It is imperative that you establish a beginning, middle, and end to your actions. This is a hard and fast rule in approaching any type of audition. You are, in a sense, performing a complete, short scene for the camera. Perhaps shuffling through papers on the side, maybe a searching scratch of the head or a sudden discovery of an idea starts your improvisation. Move to a committed, specific typing of the text as the middle of your pantomime. Button (or end) the exercise with hitting the enter key and registering a subtle look of satisfaction on your face. Such choices and invention will make for a more interesting, committed audition.

Other commercials will have copy or dialogue. Unless it is unusually long or technical (in which case it may be found on the fax services the night before), the text will not be available until you arrive at your audition. Your agent or manager will be told that the spot includes dialogue, so arrive early enough to work on it. Be very precise with your choices with regard to whom you are speaking—be specific and natural. Do not be too grand or presentational in your approach. Simplicity is best. Imagine talking to one person as compared to an audience. Unless the commercial calls for a hardcore salesman, don't pitch the information. Find a way to naturally incorporate the sometimes-technical jargon into an unforced, believable conversation. Be conscious of being likeable, warm, and approachable. Create a sense of warmth, fun, and sincere energy on camera as well as in the audition room.

Should the spot dictate that you work with a partner, it is important to develop an instant relationship with the other actor and project that to the camera. The goal here is to be in the moment and be real while at the same time having the rapport. Be genuine and believable. Many times casting calls for a husband and wife situation; if you can show the ease and familiarity that a married couple have, then that will make your audition all the more specific and notable. Find an attractive quality about the other actor that resonates with you. Go to a corner and run over the lines with your partner. Get a flow and a consistency going.

Audition Techniques

Relaxation—in both theatrical and commercial auditions, the first technique to employ is relaxation. You can't work at your optimum level if you are stiff and nervous. Your emotional channels will be blocked and your performance will be stilted, self-conscious, and uninspired. Take the time before you go into the room to breathe, relax, and center yourself. Find a deserted corner or empty hallway and go through a few short exercises. Concentrate on your face—go through a short routine of tensing and relaxing the muscles. Not only will it calm you, it will put a glow on your skin. Be sure that your mouth is mobile and flexible. Run through a few alliterative exercises to get it fully working. You don't want to have a mush mouth when you should be articulating the copy to its fullest extent. Move down to your neck and shoulders—notorious carriers of extraneous tension. Shrug your shoulders up and down while circling your neck. Finally, grow aware of your diaphragm—it is the engine of your energy and the source of your vocal power. It's a muscle. Flex it. Always make certain you are breathing from there; it will center you and free your throat from constriction. You may think this is a waste of time or some "new age" nonsense, but it is, in fact, essential to correct relaxation.

The Copy Breakdown—read the copy through at least three times in order to be clear about the parameters.

- *Tone*—note the style of the copy. Is it Realistic? Skewed? Satiric?
- *Buzz Words*—pick out the crunchy, juicy, fresh words that you can make sound like themselves and create desire to buy the product. This is not to say that you should punch or distort the word. Just recognize the onomatopoeic characteristics and inject a little flair into it.
- *Type*—is it a situational spot? A hard-sell spot? Your approach will vary depending.

The Question Technique—this is where you create a specific character by asking questions about you and your relationship to the copy. Similar to technique work done in acting classes, this is a process adapted specifically for commercials.

- *Who Are You?* Are you a past suffer of pain; doctor or nurse; athlete; businessman/woman; mom; dad? Be specific.
- *Where Are You?* At the office; home; backyard; park; beach? Be attentive to the details of all things around you in your space.
- *What is the message?* What is the main point of the commercial? How is it delivered? Subtly or emphatically?

- *Why Are You Saying This?* Are you a professional; nurse or doctor; a recovered sufferer; spokesperson? Create the reality in your head.
- *Who Are You Talking To?* Parent; child; friend; boss; employee? Being precise about this will color how you speak.

Substitution—another technique to employ is substitution. Take a line like "I love JB's burgers." Perhaps you do not like meat but you love chocolate cake. You can *think* chocolate instead of burger and *say* burger. By thinking of something you actually like, you will be positive in your approach, expression and performance. Attempt a little bit of sensory recall about the texture and smell and taste of the chocolate cake. Conjure up a memory of eating the cake—a birthday party or special dinner. The enjoyment will naturally register on your face. However, if you have a severe dislike for certain food, do let your agent know. Often the commercial requires you to eat the product—if you're a hard-core vegetarian, perhaps a gig with JB's Burgers is not the best spot for you.

The Moment Before—this technique can be most beneficial in rooting you in specificity. What just happened before your first line? What were the circumstances? Again, let's use "I love JB's burgers." Ask yourself why you're saying this. Did someone just ask about your favorite food? Or perhaps how you rate popular fast food restaurants? Who asked it? Your mom, your spouse, your children, an opinion survey? This exercise helps you set up the copy by giving yourself a complete back-story.

The Moment After—this is also important. Many times, the copy will end and you can feel free to improvise or carry on a conversation if there are two or more people in the scene. It's a skill that needs to be developed because it lets the casting director (and if in a callback—the director, producer, and clients) know that you not only have a firm grasp on the acting process but that you also can think on your feet. Other times, especially in a comedy spot, there will be a final tag line. Decide how to deliver it memorably—make it your own. If the end shot calls for just a reaction, be clever and clear about the moment. It's the last thing the auditors will see on your section of tape.

Improvisation—this is an invaluable skill to hone for both theatrical and commercial auditioning. Besides encouraging the freedom to be highly creative, it also expands the range and dynamic of your acting ability. In commercials especially, when it is your job to conjure atmosphere and situation in thirty seconds—usually in front of a blank wall—fluidity in improvisation can make a huge difference in who gets the job. Commercial workshops delve into the process of improvisation, but the study shouldn't end there. Take a class in improvisation by itself—most large cities have comedy clubs that conduct improv seminars. Look into them.

Cue Cards

While working, whether alone or with a partner, *do not memorize the lines*. Fully familiarize yourself, stick an operative phrase or two in your head, but do not commit the pages to memory. Unlike a theatrical audition where you have leeway to rehearse and memorize, the time you have with commercial copy is minimal. Most actors try to impress the casting director by having the dialogue memorized but they end up trying to remember the copy and are not able to act at all. They end up leaving the acting out, which is 50% of the work. Once in the audition room there will be a cue card with the copy clearly printed in bold magic marker situated on an easel next to the camera. Use it. If you memorize the copy, it is almost impossible to use the cue cards to help you out if you forget memorized lines. Instead, develop the skill of cue card reading.

Like reading a teleprompter, mastering the cue card is a knack that has to be polished. As the casting director or camera operator is collecting paperwork and setting up for the slate, peruse the cue card. Make sure the easel is clearly in your line of vision. It is perfectly permissible to ask the auditor to move the card to where it works best for you. See where the words fall on the poster board. Usually if there are two or more people speaking in the spot, the casting director will have the character's lines in different colors to separate the dialogue for you. Note your color—your eye will keep going back to it. Be aware, too, that the copy is sometimes not exactly the same as it was on the page you got when you walked in the office. Last-minute revisions will end up on the cue card that didn't make it to the mimeographed audition pages—another reason not to memorize. Make sure you incorporate the updates.

After you identify yourself on tape—called the slate—the camera will pause. Use the time to take a deep breath and study the cue card once more. Once the camera is rolling again, you may feel as though your eyes are shifting from the camera to the cue card and back again when you are auditioning, but it is not as noticeable as you might think. Besides, it is expected behavior—every auditioning actor is basically doing the same thing. Try to stay with the lens as much as you can; at a natural break, go back to the card and grab the next line. It takes practice, but in time you will get the feel and ability to use a cue card and make your copy combine effortlessly with your acting.

Practice makes perfect in the commercial game. Work on all the techniques; see which works especially well for you. Take it all in. Then relax and let it go.

CHAPTER NINE

The Audition

There is a standard protocol to every commercial casting office in America. Certain adaptations are made from big city to small town, but the parameters are pretty much the same. If you live in a small town where the acting opportunities for television commercials are limited, you may often find out about jobs coming to the area in the local newspaper. A casting director from a large city will arrange for a notice to be placed announcing a call to find new talent. If there is a talent agent in town, the casting director will work with that office to find actors. As for the big cities of Los Angeles, Chicago, and New York, it is best to have an agent. Agents are aware of all the auditions being held and have a relationships with casting directors to help get you an appointments to audition.

Realize that in a large city there are hundreds of actors that fit in your age category. Since a casting director can usually see no more that sixty people in one category a day, you have been given a huge opportunity. If you are unable to make your appointment, let your agent contact the casting director. Always follow protocol. Calling yourself may set a negative into action.

The Audition Session

When you get to the site of your audition, there will usually be a few rooms where sessions are being conducted. Normally, there will be a large board at the entrance of the studio announcing which room is assigned which audition. Outside each audition room will also be a board with the name of the specific commercial being cast. Underneath that will be a sign-in sheet called Exhibit E asking for your name, Social Security number, and time of audition. Your Social Security number is used for identification when the sign-in list is sent to the signatory company (usually the advertising agency) to chart overtime concerns and to SAG for record keeping only. Because of security reasons, more and more actors are leery of writing their Social Security numbers on the sign-in sheet. Some people used to choose instead to put their SAG identification numbers on that line. This is no longer a viable alternative, as signatories and SAG could not work together on the issue. So, use your Social Security number, as there is no alternative that would allow you to receive any due overtime payment unless you provide it at the time you sign in.

EXHIBIT E
SAG/AFTRA
COMMERCIAL AUDITION REPORT

PAGE _____ OF _____

TO BE COMPLETED BY CASTING DIRECTOR

(X) WHERE APPLICABLE
ON CAMERA ☐

PRINCIPAL PERFORMER ☐
OFF CAMERA ☐

EXTRA PERFORMER ☐
TELEVISION ☐   RADIO ☐

AUDITION DATE

INTENDED USE

UNION: SAG ☐   AFTRA ☐

Person to whom correspondence concerning this form shall be sent:
(Name & Phone Number)

CASTING REPRESENTATIVE NAME

COMMERCIAL TITLE - NAME & NUMBER

ADVERTISER NAME

PRODUCT   JOB NUMBER   ADVERTISING AGENCY AND CITY

PRODUCTION COMPANY

INSTRUCTIONS: Circle the name of principal performer if known.

* SPANISH LANGUAGE TRANSLATION SERVICES

TO BE COMPLETED BY PERFORMERS

NAME (PRINT)	*	SOCIAL SECURITY OR MEMBERSHIP NUMBER	AGENT (PRINT)	ACTUAL CALL	TIME IN	TIME OUT	INITIAL	CIRCLE INTERVIEW NUMBER	SEX (X) M	F	AGE (X) +40	-40	ETHNICITY (X) AP	B	C	LH	I	PWD (X)
								1st 2nd 3rd 4th										
								1st 2nd 3rd 4th										
								1st 2nd 3rd 4th										
								1st 2nd 3rd 4th										
								1st 2nd 3rd 4th										
								1st 2nd 3rd 4th										
								1st 2nd 3rd 4th										
								1st 2nd 3rd 4th										
								1st 2nd 3rd 4th										
								1st 2nd 3rd 4th										
								1st 2nd 3rd 4th										
								1st 2nd 3rd 4th										
								1st 2nd 3rd 4th										

The recorded audition material will not be used as a client demo, an audience reaction commercial, for copy testing or as a scratch track without payment of the minimum compensation provided for in the Commercials Contract and shall be used solely to determine the suitability of the performer for a specific commercial.

AUTHORIZED REPRESENTATIVE SIGNATURE _____

The only reason for requesting information on ethnicity, sex, age, and disability is for the talent unions to monitor applicant flow. The furnishing of such information is on a VOLUNTARY basis. The Authorized Representative's signature on this form shall not constitute a verification of the information supplied by performers.

Asian/Pacific — AP   Latino/Hispanic — L
Black — B   Native American — I
Caucasian — C   Performer with Disability — PWD

Mail top copy to SAG OR AFTRA on the 1st and 15th of each month.

WHITE-UNION

Posted on the board will also be a notice informing you whether you need to fill out a size card and have a Polaroid taken. The size card will ask personal information, agent's name and number, and your physical stats. Although a home phone number is important to list, again, for security reasons, some casting offices are beginning to omit home address requests. Casting sheets have a habit of ending up in an alley dumpster at the conclusion of a casting session and possibly falling into the hands of an unethical individual. Use your own discretion about giving out your home address; this is where a post office box number can be used instead.

The Polaroid is only a reference tool and although they usually aren't particularly flattering, don't worry— actors are not judged on their Polaroids. The size card and Polaroid are employed for callbacks, collating pairs or groups, and also, should you book the job, used by the production company for initial costuming information. Some casting offices choose to take a digital photograph of you from the video camera itself, print it out, and then staple it to your paperwork right before you are put on tape. This is a decided relief to many Polaroid-hating actors.

§ stuart stone casting
323 866 1811

Name

Date

Phone

Address

Agent

Agent Phone

Seen For

Are you a SAG member?

Will you work as an extra?

Social Security Number

Suit/Dress   Shirt/Bust

Inseam   Shoe

Age (if under 18)

Height   Waist

Weight   Hips

Hair   Eyes

Office Use Only

If there is ad copy, take it to a place where you can work on it. Should you have questions about the text, ask the session runner. Often outside the door there is a storyboard posted which may help clarify the action and demeanor of the spot. Study it. If the copy has two roles, and you fit both categories, be familiar with both— sometimes you are called upon to switch roles inside the audition room. If you are paired with someone, introduce yourself and work on the copy together. Develop an easy rhythm with your partner, concentrating on picking up your cues so the conversation flows smoothly and effortlessly.

You will be called in to audition from the sign-in sheet, so make sure that you signed in legibly and that you can hear your name being called. If you go outside to work on your copy, inform the person running the session of your whereabouts and get an idea of how long it might be before you are called so you can be back in time.

Once in the room, you will see there is nothing grand or glamorous going on—just a camera, some video recording equipment, lights, as well as chairs, couches, and tables for the casting director and session runner to sit and work at. Don't let the cold, machine-dominated feel of the room intimidate or throw you.

Many casting directors have an assistant or session runner who runs the camera and helps in the audition studio. Sometimes the casting director is not in the room and may be watching the auditions from a monitor in their office or another room. Session runners have substantial clout with the casting director so it's not a bad idea to try to buddy up with them in a way that does not seem pushy or fake—be natural and be yourself. When you become friendly with them, they may give you an extra take if you did not feel great about your first; they will also tell you honestly if your work was good or not. Some even have the ability to recommend you to other casting directors they work with.

You may often meet the casting director if they are in the room. Remember that they have brought you in and want to see you book the job—for them and yourself. They believe you are what the part calls for and they are rooting for you; otherwise you would not be there. But be aware they are, at this point, under a time constraint to cast the role you are being seen for. Often they are given only one day to see everyone possible for the job. Commercials move very quickly; from the time of your first audition it is usually less than two or three weeks until the shoot day and often no time to recast if the best person has not been found for the role. Casting directors are trying to see as many people as possible and need to move actors in and out of the audition. They may also simultaneously be setting up another day to see actors for other parts, or negotiating and booking talent for jobs just cast. Juggling so many tasks may make them feel stressed, agitated or any other negative emotion you may pick up. *Do not* let it affect you. No matter what you may feel, it is not directed personally at you. Do your job. You were called in because they liked your look or know your talent. What goes on tape is all that the director and ad agency will see—the casting director's attitude will not be realized. Let your talent show.

Be prepared to make the casting director's day a little easier by having your materials—8x10, resumé, size card and Polaroid—ready when you go into the session room. Do not wait until you get into the room to start getting them out.

In auditions, some actors experience a rush of nerves that can display itself in twitching, moving hands and feet, or a rocking of the body; sometimes you may ramble on or blurt out something you would ordinarily never say. This is normal when you are just starting out and the more auditions you go on, the more comfortable you will become while doing them. If you have been auditioning for a long time and nervousness still overcomes you, it may be advisable to see your audition on tape. If you have built a relationship with a casting director you might ask if such nervousness is detectable, or even ask to see your audition played back, if there is time. The best solution is to attack the problem by getting into a commercial workshop.

Pay strict attention to any of the directions given to you by the casting director or session runner. Sometimes commercials can be very technical—product placement, movement, tone, where to focus, and blocking all need to come together.

You are ahead of the game if you know that the audition starts even before the actual spot begins—with the slate. When you stand in front of the camera and state your name, and perhaps show your left and right profiles, the client and director are already watching you for likeability, ease, and personal expression. Oftentimes inexperienced actors may think they are being animated and expressive in the slate when in reality, they are listless and flat. This is where hours logged in a commercial workshop are invaluable—seeing yourself on camera can be an enlightening experience. You are selling yourself from the moment that camera begins rolling—do not waste an opportunity to show what you've got to offer from the very start.

Skills To Develop

Be clear and concrete about the situation you are acting out—in most auditions there is only you and the blank area in which you are working. Create a tangible time and place. Not only will this help you put genuine feeling into what you are saying, but will also make your choices more specific.

If there are other actors, create a relationship with them— when two or more actors work well together it brings a recognizable reality to the situation. Rather than just randomly bouncing lines back and forth, develop a rapport and timing with your partner before going into the session room. This ability is very important and makes for a memorable audition.

Have stories ready—if there is no copy, the casting director will usually ask a question of each actor to get an insight into that particular performer's personality. As discussed in Chapter Eight, practice with questions like the favorite tuna sandwich. Favorite vacation, first date, or hometown tales are also good bets. Plan a beginning, middle, and end to your stories.

Be in the moment—make precise and distinct decisions about what is happening around you. Be open to your inner voice or what the other actor is giving you. Many times what happens spontaneously is the most exciting.

Audition Reminders

Make sure your body is loosened up. It will help you get out of your head. When you are tense and stressed you are not loose.

Have fun and remember to listen.

Turn off cell phones and beepers. It is rude and embarrassing to have them go off during your audition.

Be yourself and bring yourself to the role.

Extra Work

There is a question near the bottom of the fill-out form at nearly every commercial audition—"Will you do extra work?" If you are new to the business, extra work may be a good way for you to see what goes on in the production of a commercial. However, if your focus is on being the principal actor, concentrate on that because when you take an extra job you may miss an audition for a principal role. When this happens too many times, it can conflict with your goal to be a principal actor. Should you audition for a principal role and be called for an extra part, it may not be a bad idea to take the work if you can. The production and director do not discriminate—they see actors as actors. If you were part of the original audition, they understand why you would take extra work. Also, in a best-case scenario, if another actor is needed in a scene, you may be upgraded to that part. And for many actors, extra work can help them get the few extra dollars needed to reach the required amount to get their SAG medical insurance.

Keep in mind, though, that extra work can be somewhat degrading to one's ego—you will not be getting the same treatment as the principal actor. Usually if there are two or three extras slated for a shoot, you will share a dressing room—if there is one left. When there is a big group and spacing is cramped, you will be kept in a holding area. Extras are given a hot meal like everyone else, unless it is a huge call—like a crowd scene in a stadium—in which case you will be given a box lunch. There would not be enough time to feed you any other way. Extras normally eat last and may not have a snack table called Craft Services. Bring snacks with you. You will need to keep your energy up and may go for long periods of time without being fed on the set.

There are no perks except for the SAG overtime, meal penalty bumps, and extra pay for working in various conditions. If you are a SAG member, the rate could be better than temp work or waiting tables—and you get the free meals. The rate is lower for non-union actors, but you still may want to do it for the experience of being on a set.

Should you opt to do some extra work, be professional. Besides being the right thing to do, it can benefit you personally as well. Those who have a good attitude and are friendly and outgoing to the production people are more likely to get the best positions in the scene being shot. That enhances the possibility of getting upgraded to a more prominent role—which is what most extras hope for. There is no reason to bring a negative attitude with you. You decided to work as an extra, so enjoy the experience.

After the Session

No audition is ever wasted. Stop now and repeat that axiom aloud to yourself: **no audition is ever wasted.** Auditions are stepping-stones to your commercial future—you can learn from each and every one of them. When you get to your car, or jump on the subway, you will think of several different ways you could have done the audition; perhaps you were all set to do it one way and it inadvertently came out another. Maybe you said something goofy in the interview, or seriously screwed up the copy. Even if you were brilliant, you will act it all out over and over and replay it in your head. This is all normal. So don't fight the impulse. Look at what was missing, why things went the way they did and how you can possibly change your approach. However, do *not* let your emotions run amok and do *not* beat yourself up over your perceived shortcomings. Decide objectively what you can learn from the experience—weighing both the pros and cons—and then *let it go*. Occupy yourself with an activity, go to a movie, or see some friends. There will be another day and another audition.

Callbacks

If you are selected for a callback, you will usually hear within a week—usually less. Sometimes at your initial audition, the callboard will list when the callbacks are scheduled, along with the proposed shooting dates. Should you go in again, you will see the director and the people from the advertising agency (creative director, writer, and producer). No matter how many people are crowded into the room, focus your attention on the director. He or she is in charge this time around.

There may be many reasons that you are brought back as one of the selected few. Look, performance, personality, or type may have contributed in your return. Regardless, the powers that be have decided that you might be able to fit the role that they are casting. This is not the time to let your nerves get the best of you. You will need to stay out of your head and be prepared to take direction and redirection from the director while you are in the session. If the director has you change the way you are reading or doing things, do not be concerned that this is because you are doing it the wrong way. Perhaps your range is being investigated; maybe the concept of the commercial has altered since your original audition. Do not let it throw you or adversely affect your audition. When you stay in your head, you lose all ability to act, your timing is off and bad or inappropriate choices are made. Once again, just as in a theatrical audition, work in the moment and be very clear on your acting choices.

Before you go in, fully arm yourself by focusing, taking calming deep breaths, and pulling from advice in this book. It is generally important to wear the same clothes and hairstyle you did on the original call. However, in today's market, it has become a little lax. Still, it is best to come in as you did before. If a Polaroid or digital picture was taken on the first call and the director and agency uses it on the callback you will match up. It is not a huge mistake if your wardrobe is not the same but if you came in casual clothes formal attire is not a good idea. Never change your hairstyle from your original audition and callback.

After the callback, the finalists—usually the first choice actor and a back-up choice—will be put on a hold. The callback tapes are sent to a few more decision-makers (most often the client big-wigs) for a final approval of chosen talent. Within a day or two you will find out if you booked the job. If you did, yahoo and congratulations! Good work! If you didn't, what we said before still applies—*do not beat yourself up*. You may have given a great audition but things such as age, type, not matching up well with the other actors—even hair color—may have been factors. Do not take it personally. Just take the experience and move forward. Your job is coming.

CHAPTER TEN

The Personal Pep Talk

The life of an actor can be a stimulating and rewarding one. You have the opportunity to use your entire being—everything you are, know, and feel—to become a character involved in a story that enlightens the human condition. The commercial actor, too, can claim to be a part of this noble tradition. Yes, okay, your main objective may be to hawk the wares that the client is selling, but you are still using your unique talents to accomplish that.

The acting profession differs from other professions because a great deal of the actor's life is spent interviewing for a job. Most of the population interviews for employment a few times during his or her lifetime and then stays with that job for years—maybe even an entire working life. True, some fortunate actors can get a role on a television series that may last for a few years, but for the most part, actors are journeymen who go from job to job to job—if they're lucky! This is especially true for the commercial actor. When you book a job, the shoot usually lasts only a day or two. Then it's back to square one with more auditioning. This routine can be very wearying and sometimes downright debilitating for many actors. Auditioning and performing fears need to be addressed and conquered; disappointment and rejection have to be reckoned with; self-esteem must be constantly bolstered. Dealing with these issues is every bit as vital as the concentration reserved for the usual acting, dancing, singing, and commercial classes.

Neutralizing Your Fears

Approach every interview or audition the same way: arrive at the location at least fifteen minutes ahead of your scheduled time. If you live in a large city with a network of unpredictable streets and highways such as Los Angeles, plan accordingly. Get out your *Thomas Guide* or Yahoo.com computer map and plot your travel. Allow for traffic jams and roadwork. Keep a supply of coins for parking. If you're in New York City or Chicago, take into account the unpredictability of subway and bus travel. When you get to your audition, find a place nearby where you can compose yourself—your car, a quiet coffee house, a park bench. Take deep breaths and calm any apprehensions you might have.

Even the simplest commercial audition can make the heart race a little fast and your adrenaline pump. Nerves are the natural enemy of the actor—they short-circuit your instrument. Clear your mind of all extraneous thoughts—what you have to do the rest of the day, money problems, the argument you had with your lover, your mounting laundry pile. Visualize the room where the audition is taking place; picture yourself as secure, calm, and collected. The people auditioning you are not the enemy—see them as people who would love for you to get the job, because in truth, they would. They want you to be terrific because then their job is done. Embrace the video camera as a friend, not an x-ray machine.

Rejection

Rejection is a constant reality for the actor. Whether you are a veteran or a beginner, you will always, always, always be rejected more than you are hired. That's simply the nature of the game. It's painful and it's unfair and it's depressing. But if you focus on the rejection, the rejection will immobilize you. You have to develop a way to work through the disappointment and still hold onto your self-esteem; otherwise your acting career will be mottled with debilitating bouts of anger, second-guessing, and despair.

Sometimes rejections are easy to brush off; other times you desperately want that national spot or that television role. Allow yourself a grieving period for the loss. Get mad. Throw something. Pound the walls. Shed a tear or two. Write down what you are feeling. Hit the gym. Jog around the block. *And then let it go.* Don't let it control you. You have a choice to move on. Do it.

If you are able, use the opportunity not as an indication of failure but as a chance for self-improvement. Is there anything you should have or could have done differently? Was there something that kept you from operating at your full potential? Were you not as prepared as you should have been? If so, take positive steps to correct these shortcomings. On the other hand, realize too that you might have done everything exactly right in that audition room, and the fact of the matter was that you were simply not right for the part. All actors feel deep down that if they ply their craft correctly, they should be able to play every part. But in commercials especially, many times a certain look is what is required. A readily identifiable type. You could be Meryl Streep in there, and if they want someone with a Kathie Lee Gifford look, you're not going to get the job. Accept that sometimes not getting cast has absolutely nothing to do with you.

Many actors find that being in a steady acting class helps them deal more successfully with rejection. Not only is the classroom a place where you can continue to hone your talent, but your fellow students can also provide a sympathetic support group.

Goals

Goal-setting is a very valuable tool and is extremely helpful in the process of getting what you want. Many people wander through life without a clear destination (goal) or direction (plan). This is fine for some, but for those of you who want more from your career, it's a good idea to assess where you are and where you want to ultimately end up. Goals are like stepping-stones you need to negotiate—each one leading logically to the desired final destination. The path must be followed. There are no short cuts. For example, if you do not have a car and your goal is to drive across America, unless you want to schlep by Greyhound bus, your first aim would be to get a car. When that is accomplished, then you can set your sights on the extended goal—driving across the country.

Many actors find it informative to concretely chart their dream. To see it written down somewhere in black and white. The following pages—a sort of wish-fulfilling journal—will help you with your goals. Let them be the practiced path to your success.

Once you have written all your goals out, you will realize the first three categories form a foundation that supports the base for your master goal statement. When you write your master goal statement you will be focused on the three and five-year goals as you combine your long-range goals. This is something you may want to keep in a journal or date book next to your bed, in your car, or any place that will remind you to stay focused on achieving your goals. As you write this, keep your goals in the positive. Positive affirmations are always much stronger than negative. The following is an example of what a master goal statement might look like.

> **I am a successful actor making over $500,000 a year working in commercials, television, and film, living in a three bedroom house (over 2500 square feet) with a pool, driving a BMW (over $50,000) and am in a positive cash flow without debt and am healthy, happy, and thankful.**

The reality check of the diagramming will make it clear to even the most starry-eyed aspiring performer how the flow naturally works—why, for instance, there's no going from being a working actor in thirty days to having your own show in one year without first having pictures taken and securing an agent.

Your long-range goal is the big picture—becoming a working actor, owning a home, getting married, maybe even winning an Academy Award. Then go through your time slots step by step and fill them in as the structure dictates. In thirty days you might put down meeting some photographers, booking a photo shoot, and signing up for a commercial workshop. In three months perhaps you might write down signing with a top commercial agent, going on two auditions a week, and sending postcards to casting directors.

To fully experience the power of this exercise, when entering all your aspirations, remember not to hold back. Do not compromise—be bold. Shoot for the moon. Put down everything, *everything* you want for yourself and your career. Your first step in obtaining your goals is believing that you can do it. When they are down on paper in your own handwriting they stop being pipe dreams and become your obtainable goals.

Here are a few things to keep in mind.

Be expansive with your dreamscape—scribble down everything you desire in all aspects of your life: career, relationship, financial, health/body, spiritual, educational, and family.

One goal should not contradict any of your other goals— if your financial goal is to make $60,000 a year, then don't also have a goal of buying a new $80,000 car every year. Logic should have a firm place in your structure.

State your goal in the positive rather than the negative— say what you want, not what you don't want. The statement has more power that way.

Be very specific and define your goal in detail—should you desire a home, describe it clearly (1800 square feet, three-bedroom Spanish-style bungalow, attached garage, swimming pool in the yard on a bluff overlooking the ocean).

Set high goals—do not sell yourself short.

These are my goals for...

30 Days:

Three Months:

<u>Six Months:</u>

<u>One Year:</u>

<u>Three Years:</u>

<u>Five Years:</u>

Master Goal Statement:

Now that you have created your goals and they are written down in a workable structure, the next step is utilizing them. Get into the practice of reading your long-range goals every day—once in the morning and again at night—and stay focused on them. You are free to modify your entries as often as you want, but stay in touch with the big picture.

Visualization

A practical companion piece to goal setting is creative visualization. As actors, many of our training tools, especially sense-memory and emotional recall, are rooted in exploring and expanding our imaginations. Adapt that same process to the practical, business side of acting by becoming an expert at creative visualization. Create a mental picture of your career situation exactly as you want it. See yourself fully attaining what you desire. Believing that you can accomplish something is the first step in accomplishing it. Once you have set some reasonable goals, creative visualization can mobilize and focus you. Get in touch with the dreams you had as a kid and fashion them into an attainable reality. Visualization is like a muscle that you are developing; you have to exercise to spur mass growth. During these sessions, as with goal-setting, strive to only concentrate on positive energy—what you want (not what you don't want). If you are successful at the exercise, you will discover a drive and intent and clarity that will not only do wonders for your self-esteem, but for your career was well.

Self-Esteem

Because rejection is so prevalent for the actor, it is absolutely imperative that you maintain healthy self-esteem. You are not measured by your failings, the things you accumulate, or the amount of money you do or do not make from year to year. You are a full human being just by being human. Embrace your weaknesses as well as your strengths; celebrate your quirks as well as your normalcy; accept your physical defects as well as your physical attributes. They are what make you specifically *you.*

The one thing you have to sell as an actor that no one else has is the uniqueness of you. No one else is you; no one else is like you. Stop comparing yourself to other people. Refrain from measuring your career advancements against someone else's. Everyone is on his or her own timetable. The only comparisons that should be made are those of yourself to yourself: how have you grown over the years? What have you learned? Are you grateful for what you have, or bitter about what you don't have? Do you feel in charge of your life or a victim? Have you loved? Have you been loved in return? Is your path in life making you happy?

And when you do accomplish something—when you feel great about an audition, when you do get that callback, when you do book that job—by all means celebrate your success. We have all become masters at beating ourselves up for our failures but are woefully inept at embracing our accomplishments. Take yourself out to dinner. Buy yourself something nice. Do a little end-zone victory dance.

The great historian and myth guru Joseph Conrad says, "Follow your bliss." When all is said and done, if the acting life you've chosen is not making you happy, if you cannot find a way to work through the rejection and the disappointment, if you find yourself regretting more than find yourself rejoicing, then maybe it's time to rethink your path. Look inside and ask yourself if this is what you really want. The life of a performer is difficult enough without being constantly miserable. If you decide to stick with it, shake up your complacency. Go back on the stage. Get involved in a workshop. Do scene-study work with fellow actors. Investigate teaching. Try writing, painting, sculpturing. There are many roads on the artist's map that can ultimately lead to your bliss.

When You Aren't Booking Like You Used To

Sometimes your commercial career can be going along just fine—booking a couple commercials a year, auditioning consistently. And then there can be periods where you suddenly feel that you have gone a bit cold. You aren't getting callbacks. Maybe you aren't auditioning as much as you used to. There can be many reasons why this is happening.

Perhaps you've gone stale or gotten bored in your auditions—like you're on automatic pilot. This can translate as being flat and uninteresting in your interviews—death for the commercial actor. When this happens, it's not unusual that you're feeling the same way about your emotional and personal life as well. Do something to shake up your creative juices. Re-examine the reason you wanted to go into acting and commercials to begin with.

Or perhaps you find yourself falling out of one category—teen or young adult—and moving into a less in-demand category (sometimes, for some people, the 30s can be tough). When that happens, some actors, unfortunately, begin trying too hard, overcompensating, looking and feeling a bit desperate.

Use this chance to re-invent yourself. Get some on-camera coaching and see what's missing. Adjust your appearance a bit. Maybe put a rinse on your hair—or let the gray show through. Get yourself some new pictures. Pare down and sharpen your resumé. If you feel like your agents have lost interest in representing you, maybe begin looking around for other representation.

The point is to be active about your situation. Don't be a victim. Never give away your personal power. Rediscover that spark, that passion, that likeability, that energy that made you commercially viable before.

CHAPTER ELEVEN

Booking the Job, Contract Issues, On-Set Etiquette

When all of the personal application, concentration, talent and luck come together with the right commercial and part, you will get the job. The casting director will call your agent with a booking and confirm the rate you will be paid and the dates you will be working. When the business details are all worked out, and your agent phones you with the good news, make sure you do something to celebrate your achievement. Reward yourself with a gift; take a friend out to dinner; send a vase of flowers to your agent. We're not suggesting that you blow your bank account out, but make the occasion special, because it is.

Before your euphoria wanes, the wardrobe department from the production company hired to shoot the commercial will be calling you directly to handle all costuming issues. Most often your agent will have reached you before the costumer calls, but in the fast-paced world of commercials, sometimes it happens that wardrobe gets to you first. If you have not heard from the agent, ask the wardrobe person for their number and call your agent for your booking verification and then call the wardrobe person back. A call from the wardrobe person is not a conformation of you getting the job; wait until you hear it directly from your agency. The costume designer will ask your sizes, and depending on the shoot, question you on the possibility of perhaps using some articles of your own personal clothing. An appointment will be scheduled for a fitting.

At this point you need to make sure your agent has given the production company all your current contact numbers: home, cell, and beeper. The production unit should be able to reach you without any hassle and within a five-minute time period. They will appreciate your effort in making their job a little less stressful. With all they have to do, the last thing they need is to concentrate on tracking you down for hours at a time.

The Fitting

The next step is usually the fitting. This is done at the production office or hotel or any place that will accommodate the space and parade of people. You will show the clothing and accessories that the wardrobe person asked you to bring; there will be other clothes in your size at the fitting as well. You will then try on several selections and the director and advertising agency people will decide what looks right and works best for the commercial. Polaroids will be taken of you in each of your ensembles. If the decision is made that your own clothes will be used, you will be reimbursed according to SAG and AFTRA guidelines. Make sure to leave the designated articles of clothing with the wardrobe people. There have been many times when the wardrobe people have let actors take their clothes home with them and then the day of the shoot the clothes are forgotten at home. Leaving your clothes with wardrobe ensures that the clothes will be there when you get to the set or location for the shoot. You will meet many people—besides the costumer and director there will be assistants and production liaisons and clients—and it will be hard to remember everyone. Just smile and be as friendly as you can. Repeating a person's name to yourself after meeting them can be beneficial. Be aware that the fitting session can sometimes run an hour or two. Clients especially can be maddeningly exact about the look they want to best show off their product. Do not complain. Do not protest. Most of the people making decisions on your wardrobe chose you and were rooting for you and are happy to have you in their commercial. Don't make them wish they had gone with their second choice instead. When you are finished with your fitting and everyone is satisfied with your apparel, you will be asked to sign out. The production company needs to keep track of how long the session was, because you will be paid for your time.

Before you leave wardrobe, make sure you get a call sheet and a map to the location if it is available. If the location and/or call time have not been finalized, make sure the production assistants have current numbers to call you with your call time and shoot location. The people who phone with this information are usually harried and multi-tasking; you need to make reaching you as easy as possible for them. They should have all your numbers (beeper, work, fax, cell, home). For your part, ask for the producer's name and the 2nd AD's name and numbers to reach them in case of an emergency. Your agent will probably also have these numbers, but it is a good business practice to have them listed in your day planner as well. Always try to let your agent deal directly with the production company and 2nd AD. However, let's say if you are on your way to the set and it's 4am and you get a flat you would call the producer to let him know you will be late. When they are apprised of your situation, they will be able to help you or try to work around your shot until you show up to the set.

CALL SHEET

Production Co.

PRODUCT:	Sunrise:	LOCATION:
CLIENT:	Sunset:	
Address:	16mm: MOS:	
Phone:	35mm: x SYNC: x	
Fax:		PARKING:
Personnel:		
AGENCY: Calltime: EDITOR:		CONTACT NUMBERS - CELL:
Address: Address		Katy / Prod. Super
Phone / Fax: Phone / Fax:		CHRISTINE/Asst. Prod.Sup
Personnel: Personnel:		PAUL/ LOCATONS
		MOHO FAX:

C R E W

CATEGORY	NAME:	PHONE #:	OTHER #:	CALL	OUT	CATEGORY	NAME:	PHONE #:	OTHER #:	CALL	OUT
DIRECTOR						LEADMAN					
MANAGING DIRECTOR						SET DRESSER					
EXEC. PROD.						JET SETS GM					
PRODUCER						PROP MASTER					
1st ASST DIR.						PROP ASST.					
2nd ASST DIR.						STYLIST					
PROD. SUPERVISOR						ASSISTANT STYLIST					
ASST PROD SUPER						MAKEUP					
DIRECTOR OF PHOTOG						SCRIPT SUPERVISOR					
1ST A.C.						VTR					
2ND A.C.						SOUND					
LOADER						BOOM OPERATOR					
GAFFER						GANG BOSS					
BB ELEC/ DRIVER						PRODUCTION TRAILER					
3RD ELECTRIC						TALENT TRAILER					
ELECTRIC						PA- Production Truck					
4TH ELECTRIC						PA- Camera Truck					
KEY GRIP						PA- Stakebed					
BB GRIP/ DRIVER						PA					
3RD GRIP						PA					
4TH GRIP						PA					
GRIP DRIVER						SNACK ARTIST					
PRODUCTION DESIGN						LOCATION MANAGER					
ART COORDINATOR						LOCATION ASST.					
SET DECORATOR						CATERER - BREAKFAST					
						CATERER - LUNCH					

T A L E N T

ROLL:	NAME:	PHONE #:	OTHER#:	CALL	OUT	AGENCY:	AGENT NAME:	PHONE #:	OTHER#:	CALL	OUT
HERO WOMAN											
TELEPHONE POLE MAN											
VESPA WOMAN											

E Q U I P M E N T

ITEM:	VENDOR:	PHONE #:	CONTACT:	CALL	OUT	ITEM:	VENDOR:	PHONE #:	CONTACT:	CALL	OUT
CAMERA						LAYOUT BOARD					
CASTING						LIGHTING					
CASTING FACILITY						MESSENGER					
CATERER - BREAKFAST						PAYROLL					
CATERER - LUNCH						PERMITS					
CELL PHONES						PRODUCTION MOHO					
DAILIES						PRODUCTION SUPPLIES					
DOLLY						RAW STOCK					
GENERATOR						SECURITY					
GRIP EQUIPT						SET CONSTRUCTION					
HOTEL- AGENCY						SOUND					
HOTEL- DIRECTOR						TRASH BINS					
INSURANCE						VEHICLES					
JIB ARM						VTR					
LAB						WALKIES					

NOTES:

PRODUCTION SUMMARY:

FIRST SHOT AM: STOCKS:
LUNCH: CAMERA ROLL NO.'s:
FIRST SHOT PM: TOTAL FOOTAGE SHOT:
DINNER: SOUND ROLL NO.'s:
WRAP CAMERA: FILM NOTES / COMMENTS:
LAST MAN OUT:

On the Set

When you arrive on the set, report to the 2nd AD or introduce yourself to one of the people running around with a walkie-talkie. Tell them you want to let someone know you are on the set and that you need direction to where you can put your belongings. If you are on location, you might have a dressing room in a trailer (called a Honeywagon); if on a studio lot, you may be placed in a small room on a soundstage. As soon as you are situated, the 2nd AD will ask for two forms of identification (driver's license, birth certificate, passport, or Social Security card) and present you with your W-2 tax form and your contract. Make sure you sign your contract prior to going in front of the camera. Read it carefully and confirm that the deal is what you and your agent agreed upon. Is there a usage rate for cable? Internet? Any print buys? Do you have a guarantee for this commercial if it is not a national and you negotiated to be paid over SAG scale? If you had to cut or restyle your hair was it paid for and compensation added? If you find something wrong, be careful to remain calm. Pleasantly explain what you thought the deal was and that you would like to call your agent for confirmation. If there is a problem, the producer will smooth over the omissions or additions with your agent immediately— the clock is running; money dictates that the problem will be quickly resolved.

Next, you will be asked to go to wardrobe and/or makeup when those departments are set up and ready for you. Until then, there is usually a table for snacks called Craft Services and you can go there; or if there is a catering truck and they are serving food, you are usually allowed to get yourself some breakfast. Remember to pack snacks for your day on the set, as there are sometimes long periods of time between meal breaks.

Always be professional and check with someone in charge first, though. If, for any reason, you leave the area or cannot be located visually, let the 2nd AD know where you are going. It is usually best to hang close to your dressing room. If there is extensive copy, go over your lines. If not, bring a newspaper or crossword puzzles or a book to occupy yourself until you are called to the set. Keep your cell phone near—it's your only contact with the outside world for the day. Make sure to keep your phone or beeper on vibrate mode, as there is sensitive sound equipment on the set. A blaring cell phone ring could disrupt the setup.

Once on the set, be friendly and outgoing—besides the director, the costumers, make-up artists, and director of photography are especially good people to get to know—they are in charge of making you look good. The ad agency people and clients will usually be overseeing the shoot on monitors off to the side or in another room. Besides being genial with them, make sure you demonstrate your work ethic. They are, after all, paying your salary; they are your bosses. They will know when you are schmoozing them and working them over. Don't be an annoyance; be aware of what you say. Cement a good relationship with them, and they may use you again in the future. If you get on their bad side, they will never hire you again.

Shooting

Any set is notoriously crowded with technical craftsmen and women. After a few shoots you will begin to discern who does what. Remember to only take direction from the director. Should clients, producers, other well-meaning actors suggest ideas for you to explore, smile and listen, but do not act on them. It is the director's job to direct you, no one else's.

Commercials are much more technical than shooting television or films. They have more to do with hitting your marks, product placement and, especially, time issues.

Spots are usually fifteen or thirty seconds. Many times technical demands will supercede artistic choices simply to make sure that the spot fits time-wise. You may be asked to do the scene over and over until the timing or look is what the director wants. Sometimes you will be asked to speed up or slow down your delivery. This is no reason for you to abandon your creativity. You can repeat your performance, but do not fall into the trap of being mechanical. Keeping within the structure given, you can always shade your delivery a bit one way or another to keep it fresh and alive.

As in any film job, remember to stay in character until the director yells, "cut." The scene is not done until the director determines that it is. Don't make the mistake of ruining a take by assuming the shot is completed.

Signing Out

Never leave the set without being officially told that your job is finished by one of the ADs. When you are released from the set, there is a sign-out sheet to sign when you leave for the day. It has your arrival time, finishing time and meal breaks as well as fees paid to you for personal wardrobe usage. If you have been flown to a location, it will include your travel dates (for which you are paid). Make certain that all the listings are correct before you attach your signature to it. This is the report sent to the union and should there be any disagreements about payments later, it is your only verification. For instance, if you did not get a meal as timed out by SAG, then you are entitled to meal penalty payments. If you worked late, you get overtime. If you are out of town on location and you are not used on a day of shooting, you are to be paid for that day as well as for the days you traveled and actually shot. Although you are officially labeled as "talent" on the set, that doesn't mean that you should leave your business head at home.

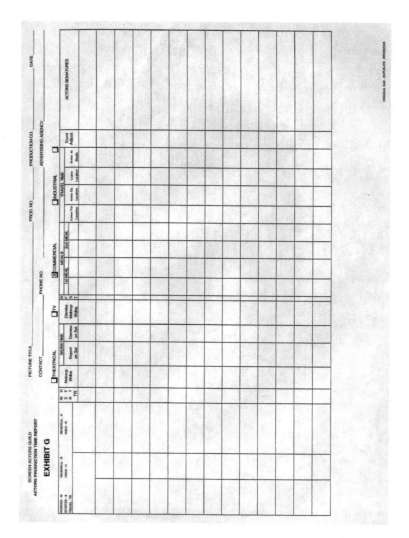

If wardrobe has any of your clothes, grab those and clean out your dressing room of all your personal belongings. Hang up any costume pieces that are not yours. Then, before you climb into your car, circle the set and thank everyone. *Everyone.* Not only is it just good manners—personal and professional—it is good business. Human nature being what it is, people like to work again with actors they know are talented and personable. You never know—the lowly assistant you struck up a friendship with might just end up in a position of power someday. Kindness and integrity—as well as talent—are remembered.

CHAPTER TWELVE

Making It Happen

Now that you have a deeper understanding of the workings of the commercial acting world, it is time to use the tools, techniques, and suggestions provided in this guidebook to fulfill your goals. We've given you the map; it is up to you to travel the road. If you believe in yourself, commit to your career, stay focused, enroll in a workshop and study this book, there is no reason why you will not reach your desired destination. Like anything else in life, success depends on how much concerted effort you put into it.

Put Down This Book and Get Out There

Remember, no one is like you. You are unique. Harness and hone that individuality into a viable commodity: a marketable and sellable actor. The ability to make a career out of commercials will depend on a winning combination of your skill, technique, likeability, directability, looks, range, and commitment. Being successful at commercials can be a wonderful and rewarding facet of being a working actor.

We wish you the best of luck and are behind you all the way.

ABOUT THE AUTHORS

To casting director **Stuart Stone**, it's the face that makes the impression—along with the acting—that uniquely defines the actor. His eye for spotting leading and emerging talent has kept him at the forefront of film, television, and commercial casting in Los Angeles for nearly a decade.

With the reputation for having an innovative and imaginative approach to the casting process, Stuart has the edge needed to fill today's widely varied commercial spots as well as spots geared toward dramatic, dialogue-driven, beauty, comedy, niche, children, sports, and any other requested markets.

Got Clio? Stuart does—as well as numerous industry accolades for his work. Not only has his tireless discovery of intriguing new actors and models earned him recognition from many top directors, his utilization of now-famous actors demonstrates his ability to successfully cast a vast array of first-class projects.

Stuart's awareness of new faces entering the market guarantees his clients the freshest look for their projects, anywhere in the world. Stuart is known for finding talent throughout the United States and worldwide—as he frequently casts talent indigenous to locations featured in a full range of projects. That kind of versatility and flexibility provides the client with the best possible cast for any given project.

Stuart's work with thousands of actors—in classroom settings, audition sessions, and guest-lecturing appearances across the country—ensures that his information is the most current, most relevant to the working professional, and the most valuable in helping the working actor make money in commercials!

For more information on Stuart and *Acting Out*, visit http://www.actingoutinfo.com.

A working Broadway, television, film, and commercial actor for over 25 years, **Dennis Bailey** is also coauthor (with David Mixner) of the recent *Los Angeles Times'* #1 Best-Selling Non-Fiction book *Brave Journeys*. He is also coauthor (with Dinah Manoff) of the play *Telegram from Heaven*, which had extended runs in Los Angeles and Chicago. An accomplished painter, Dennis lives in Venice, California, with his aloof dog, Regardless.

INDEX

OTHER TITLES FROM CRICKET FEET PUBLISHING

*Casting Qs: A Collection of
Casting Director Interviews*
by Bonnie Gillespie © 2003

*Self-Management for Actors:
Getting Down to (Show) Business*
by Bonnie Gillespie
available Summer 2003

*Casting Calendar: An Actor's
Datebook and Action Log*
by Bonnie Gillespie
available Pilot Season 2004

Acting Out Order Form

Online orders: visit http://cricketfeet.com/actingout.
Postal orders: send this form with check or money order to

> Cricket Feet Publishing
> P.O. Box 1417
> Hollywood, CA 90028

Please do not send cash.

We will send a copy of *Acting Out: Your Personal Coach to a Money-Making Career in Television Commercials* as follows:

Name: _____

Address: _____

City: _____ State: _____ Zip: _____

Telephone: _____

Email Address: _____

Price: $16.95 per copy. Please call 323.871.1331 to arrange for bulk discounts to bookstores and educational facilities.

Sales tax: please add 8.25% tax for products shipped to California addresses.

Shipping: United States: $2 for first book, $1 for each additional book; International: $8 for first book, $2 for each additional book.

Payment (in U.S. dollars):

> Check   Money Order   (circle one)

Total Enclosed: _____
- ❏ Check here if you would like to be added to our mailing list for notification of future publications, speaking engagements, and other promotional activities.